NEIGHBOUR NUISANCE,

S~~OCIAL LANDLORDS AND THE~~ LAW

ONE WEEK LOAN

PUBLISHED FOR THE JOSEPH ROWNTREE FOUNDATION

BY THE CHARTERED INSTITUTE OF HOUSING

The Chartered Institute of Housing
The Chartered Institute of Housing is the professional organisation for all people who work in housing. Its purpose is to take a strategic and leading role in encouraging and promoting the provision of good quality affordable housing for all. The Institute has more than 15,500 members working in local authorities, housing associations, the private sector and educational institutions.

Chartered Institute of Housing
Octavia House, Westwood Way
Coventry CV4 8JP
Telephone: 024 7685 1700

The Joseph Rowntree Foundation
The Joseph Rowntree Foundation has supported this project as part of its programme of research and innovative development projects, which it hopes will be of value to policy makers, practitioners and service users. The facts presented and views expressed in this report, however, are those of the authors and not necessarily those of the Foundation.

Joseph Rowntree Foundation
The Homestead
40 Water End
York YO30 6WP
Telephone: 01904 629241

Neighbour nuisance, social landlords and the law
Written by Caroline Hunter, Judy Nixon and Sigrid Shayer

© JRF/CIH 2000

Published for the Joseph Rowntree Foundation by the Chartered Institute of Housing
ISBN 1 903208 04 1

Graphic design by Jeremy Spencer
Cover illustration by Paul Johnson
Editorial management by Alan Dearling
Printed by Redwood Books

CONTENTS

CHARTS AND TABLES

ACKNOWLEDGEMENTS

We would like to thank the members of the advisory group for this project who provided support throughout and whose comments were always useful and thought provoking. They were:

  Tim Winter, Social Landlords Crime and Nuisance Group
  Bill Pitt, Manchester City Council
  Gerard Lemos, Lemos and Crane
  Steve Osborne, Safe Neighbourhoods Unit
  Ellis Blackmore, Housing Corporation
  Inspector John Piekos, Greater Manchester Police
  Pat Hayden and Laura Brennan, London Borough of Camden
  Jeanette York, Local Government Association
  Naseem Malik, Oldham M.B.C.
  Assistant Chief Constable David Swift, Staffordshire Constabulary
  Pauline Prosser, DETR
  Suzie Scott, University of Glasgow

Data collection and analysis of the individual case files was principally carried out by Susannah Greenwood. Our thanks to her.

EXECUTIVE SUMMARY

Strategic responses to anti-social behaviour can only be developed if there is an understanding of the complex nature of the problem. The research outlined in this report provides a detailed and systematic examination of the issue and addresses a number of key questions:

■ What types of behaviours are complained about?

The problem of neighbour nuisance and anti-social behaviour is difficult to classify and impossible to quantify. It is clearly a dynamic phenomenon, involving a broad range of disruptive behaviours. *"Anything, which interferes with the peaceful enjoyment of the home and surrounding area,"* was a typical summary used by one housing officer. Landlords also talk about behaviour, which make individuals or the community feel, *"threatened, vulnerable, or uneasy."*

Most commonly, complaints that led to legal action being taken concerned behaviours involving verbal abuse and noise, unruly children, harassment and violent behaviour. Respondents identified three main types of behaviour as warranting consideration for legal action:

- low level, but persistent behaviour;
- behaviour causing severe distress;
- behaviour having an adverse or potentially adverse effect on the wider neighbourhood.

■ Who are the perpetrators?

Perpetrators in serious anti-social behaviour cases were found likely to have multiple problems. More than two-thirds of defendants were described by housing officers as having particular vulnerabilities or special needs such as mental health problems or other disadvantages. High levels of poverty were also evident with 90 per cent of defendants being dependent on state benefits of some kind.

■ How big is the problem and is it increasing?

Due to deficiencies in landlords' recording, and monitoring systems, it was impossible to measure the scale of anti-social behaviour or to establish whether the problem was increasing or decreasing.

A third of local authorities (34 per cent) and over half of registered social landlords (54 per cent) failed to keep any records of the number of complaints received, and only a quarter of registered social landlords were able to provide detailed information on action taken to deal with individual cases. Usually, rather idiosyncratic recording processes were employed at the initial complaint stage, which prevented systematic monitoring of action taken. As one front line officer explained: *"everyone has their own way of doing things."*

It is clear that landlords experienced many difficulties in accurately monitoring the progress of cases. But there were also examples of good practice. Where a specialist unit or officer was employed, detailed recording and monitoring improved. One large local authority had developed a very consistent, reliable, computerised system where trends could easily be identified. Computerisation, however, was not necessarily the only tool for improvement. A specialist officer in a medium sized local authority used a manual system, which was felt to provide some safeguards over data protection problems associated with computerised records.

Notwithstanding organisations' failure to measure the incidence of anti-social behaviour, three-quarters of landlords perceived it to be a significant and increasing problem. Perceptions were effected by regional and organisational factors with landlords operating in inner city and metropolitan areas eight times more likely to see anti-social behaviour as a major problem, as compared with non-metropolitan landlords.

■ What action are landlords taking to deal with the problem?

Tenancy agreements
Generally, the changes to tenancy agreements, stimulated by the 1996 Housing Act, were seen by landlords to have made a positive contribution in preventing anti-social behaviour. Officers thought that methods of informing tenants of these changes had been very effective, however, interviews with

tenants raised some doubts over the extent to which tenancy agreements were actually read or understood.

Multi-agency partnerships

Landlords were aware of the potential benefits of joint working, but in practice, multi-agency partnerships were fraught with difficulties and were dependant on partners being prepared to understand and negotiate around different organisational cultures with different agendas and different budget limitations.

Specialist units/officers

The use of specialist units and officers whose work is primarily if not entirely devoted to implementing anti-social behaviour policies is becoming more common. Dedicated officers working alongside strengthened organisational policy and support indicate the level of the organisation's commitment as does the direction of limited resources to dealing with problems that otherwise go unreported and unchecked, but cause misery and distress for many parties. Specialist services were seen as being crucial in improving organisations' efficiency in dealing with the problems surrounding anti-social behaviour. As well as providing a more professional and committed approach, the intervention of specialist officers was valuable in providing training and support to front line officers. Those who did not have such a service would have liked to have access to one, either in-house or by buying in services from other agencies. The degree to which this was seen as useful, depended on the size of the organisation, with small organisations balancing the extent of the problem against the amount of resources required to support such a service.

■ Are existing legal remedies effective, or does eviction simply displace the problem to other housing sectors?

Eviction is the most drastic of the remedies available to social landlords for dealing with anti-social behaviour. Most landlords only took such action as a last resort when all other methods of problem resolution had been explored. The following dispute resolution methods were routinely employed:

- mediation undertaken either by an independent agency or by housing officers;
- responses to complaints involving use of letters, personal visits, in-depth investigations, use of compromise techniques, education, and support;
- on occasions, contact with tenants resulted in terminations and abandonment.

Not all cases could be resolved through such methods and over the last five years there has been a significant increase in landlords' use of legal remedies. During the period 1996-8 the number of Notices of Seeking Possession (NSPs) and possession summons issued on the grounds of anti-social behaviour had more than doubled.

The effectiveness of eviction

Contrary to landlords' perceptions that courts were unwilling to grant possession orders, an outright order was found to be the most likely outcome to possession action. It is clear that in cases involving extremely disturbing anti-social behaviour the granting of such orders could resolve major management problems on estates and ensure more efficient use of resources.

But housing officers often felt eviction was only a partially effective remedy. They noted its failure to deal with underlying causes of problem behaviour and that it frequently resulted in the problem being displaced to the private sector. With the increased diversity of providers operating in social housing estates it was not uncommon for households who have been evicted to seek tenancies in the same locality. Thus, despite regaining possession, the nuisance behaviour may continue with landlords having little control over further enforcement action, resulting in a loss of community confidence.

> *"In some cases it solves the problem but in others it doesn't because they just move to another address within the community. There are two notable cases I can think of where we've got a possession order, they've been evicted and they've moved to an adjacent street."*

The lack of use of injunctions

As an alternative to possession action, landlords can use injunctions. This remedy has the advantage of enabling action to be taken without the threat of eviction and the possible displacement of the problem.

Surprisingly, despite recent amendments strengthening the power of injunctions, very few landlords could provide any information about their use. While just under two-thirds of local authorities stated they were prepared to use injunctions, an examination of action taken in individual cases showed that in practice they were rarely employed.

The small number of organisations who regularly used injunctions were very positive about their benefits, but frequently landlords lacked the necessary knowledge or skills to use them. Commonly, landlords stated *"we have not a lot of experience in injunctions and we haven't made use of them."*

Working with the courts

Most landlords were positive about their relationships with the courts and judges, although concerns did emerge about delay, the intimidatory atmosphere of courts and inconsistent decision making from judges. In some areas it was clear that defendants did not have access to proper legal services to defend claims.

■ What action do tenants think landlords should take to control the problem?

Tenants affected by anti-social behaviour – complainants and defendants – were found to have endured prolonged periods of anxiety and stress. Their stories were often traumatic and in some cases tragic.

The complainants' perspective

Although some landlords were developing the appropriate specialist skills, all too often complainants were disappointed by the landlord's response and thought more effective action could have been taken at an earlier stage. In particular complainants criticise landlords for:

- delays in taking appropriate action;
- lack of adequate support from housing officers;
- failure to provide protection from witness intimidation and adequate witness support.

The perpetrators' perspective

Like complainants, defendants were also critical of the way in which their landlord managed the problem and were concerned about:

- lack of rigorous investigation of complaints;
- inadequate evidence collection methods employed;
- inappropriate action being taken and a failure to involve other agencies.

■ What role can introductory tenancies play?

The development of temporary introductory tenancies created much controversy when first used in 1996. At the time of the survey just under a third of local authorities had adopted introductory tenancies with a further one in ten planning to introduce them in the next 12 months. This compared to one in ten registered social landlords using starter tenancies with a further 18 per cent planning to adopt them in the next 12 months. Distinct regional variations in the use of temporary tenancies were noted.

Nearly half of the landlords using introductory tenancies had subsequently evicted tenants. How far the use of introductory tenancies can be seen as a tool being used against anti-social tenants must, however, be doubted since most cases for eviction were for rent arrears (68 per cent) rather than for neighbour nuisance (19 per cent). Landlords also expressed many concerns over their effectiveness with landlords operating in areas of low demand particularly sceptical of their value.

■ Are exclusion policies working?

It is apparent that there is a growing trend for social landlords to exclude households on the grounds of anti-social behaviour. Around a half of all social landlords, (local authorities 52 per cent: registered social landlords; 46 per cent) were found to have formal exclusion policies with nearly twice as many metropolitan authorities excluding households as compared to non-metropolitan authorities.

The criteria for exclusion varied widely between organisations, with some only taking action where tenants had been formally evicted, while others would exclude if tenants were even *suspected* of not being able to abide by the tenancy agreement. The time limit for exclusions also varied. In some organisations, tenants were effectively permanently excluded, whereas in others they could be reconsidered after a period of time.

A number of problems were noted with such policies. For example, in unpopular areas excluding households could contribute to a further weakening of demand and could result in increasing levels of empty property. Landlords were also aware that exclusion policies could have the effect of displacing the problem to the private sector.

■ The way forward

The research findings illustrate the many difficulties landlords experienced in developing effective methods of dealing with anti-social behaviour. There are now wide-ranging legal powers available to landlords to tackle neighbour nuisance. While some improvements may be required in the court management of cases, the research found little evidence to support the view that further legal reform is required. The development of strategies to deal effectively with anti-social behaviour, however, requires a greater understanding of the dynamic nature of the problem. Simple solutions are rarely sufficient. Anti-social behaviour can take many forms. Some incidents can be relatively minor, others very serious causing extreme distress and misery to many people. The underlying causes are frequently complex and behaviours are likely to change over time.

The research was carried out and this report prepared in parallel with the work of the Social Exclusion Unit's Policy Action Team 8 on anti-social behaviour. Some of the findings of this research were fed into the PAT 8 work, and many of their recommendations echo our own. Given the timing of our research, we have not been able to examine the use of anti-social behaviour orders, dealt with at greater length in the PAT report (SEU, 2000).

The research provides a useful benchmark in identifying the ways in which landlords can develop effective ways of dealing with this multi-faceted and complicated issue. However, before any further action can be taken, landlords need to develop clear procedures for recording complaints and monitoring action taken to resolve problems. Without such systems it is impossible to, establish the scale of the problem, assess whether it is increasing or decreasing, map alternative strategies and develop successful forms of intervention. Detailed recommendations arising out of the research are given at the end of the report.

CHAPTER 1

INTRODUCTION

Over recent years, neighbour nuisance and anti-social behaviour have been highlighted as a major area of concern for social landlords. This concern has found expression both through government initiatives and also increased media exposure of the issue. In the absence of reliable and accurate information on the nature of the problem, media images have moulded popular perceptions, which focus on the stereotypes of 'neighbours from hell.' The typical image portrayed is of a widespread problem involving people on council estates, with residents confirming that it only takes one bad apple to bring the whole neighbourhood into a cycle of decline and despondency. As attention has focussed on the prevalence of anti-social behaviour amongst social tenants, landlords have sought greater powers and formed a lobbying and information group (Social Landlords' Crime and Nuisance Group). In response, recent governments have strengthened landlords' powers to control the problem.

❑ Recent legislative change

The first concrete government proposals addressing the issue were contained in the Department of Environment consultation paper in 1995 entitled, *Anti-social Behaviour on Council Estates: Consultation Paper on Probationary Tenancies* (DoE, 1995). In the same year, the Labour Party (then in opposition) published its own proposals in the document, *A Quiet Life: Tough Action on Criminal Neighbours* (Labour Party, 1995).

The Conservative Party proposals were translated into legislation in the Housing Act 1996. This contained three elements which directly addressed the issue of neighbour nuisance:

i. Provision of introductory tenancies

These allow local authorities to adopt a scheme under which all new tenants of the authority are granted an 'introductory tenancy' rather than a secure tenancy. The effect of this is that if the authority wishes to evict, there is no requirement to prove any ground for possession, nor is there any discretion on the part of the judge. Certain procedural requirements, including offering an internal review of the decision to evict, must be completed before possession can be sought in the court. The introductory tenancy lasts for 12 months and providing possession proceedings have not been commenced, converts automatically to a secure tenancy after 12 months.

It should be noted that such tenancies are not available to registered social landlords. The Housing Corporation has, however, developed guidelines when dealing with 'problem' estates, for the use of assured shorthold tenancies (which similarly give minimal security), known colloquially as 'starter tenancies'.

ii. Extended grounds for possession

Tenants of social landlords are generally either secure or assured and accordingly subject to the provisions of either the Housing Act 1985 or the Housing Act 1988. To obtain possession on the basis of neighbour nuisance the landlord has to rely on a ground for possession. Both Acts contain two relevant grounds: breach of a term of the tenancy, and a specific ground relating to nuisance and illegal behaviour. The specific grounds (2 in the 1985 Act, 14 in the 1988 Act) were extended by the 1996 Housing Act. The amendments made four main changes:

- including visitors to the dwelling amongst those whose conduct was to be considered;

- including conduct 'likely to be a nuisance', so that it was not necessary to prove that anyone had actually suffered a nuisance or an annoyance and accordingly intended to make it easier to use 'professional' witnesses;

- extending those who were suffering the nuisance from *'neighbours'* to any persons *"residing, visiting or otherwise engaging in a lawful activity in the locality"*;

- adding to relevant convictions those of an arrestable offence committed in, or in the locality of, the dwelling house.

iii. New forms of injunction

Injunctions may be used by landlords to order tenants to desist from particular behaviour. One of the perceived problems with injunctions was that while tenants could be injuncted on the basis of a breach of the tenancy agreement, it was very difficult for landlords to take action against non-tenants. The 1996 Act introduced a new basis for injunctions which could be sought by local authorities against both tenants and non-tenants where the person against whom it was sought had committed or threatened to commit violence. In certain circumstances, a power of arrest could also be attached to such injunctions.

In addition, the courts were given the power to add a power of arrest to injunctions based on breach of both local authorities' and registered social landlords' tenancy agreements, again in cases of violence or threatened violence.

Less directly, the 1996 Act also made changes to the law relating to the allocation of social housing. For the first time, authorities were given the explicit power to exclude certain groups from their waiting lists. The Department of Environment (DoE) advice which followed this acknowledged (DoE/DoH, 1997, para. 4.27) that such exclusions might include those, *"with a history of anti-social behaviour"*. The Act also reduced the rights of the homeless, so that where they are housed by the authority the tenancy will be insecure for a period of up to two years, unless a waiting list offer is made.

Since the Labour Party came to power there has been a continuing preoccupation with anti-social behaviour, which has in turn led to the new 'anti-social behaviour order' (ASBO) in the Crime and Disorder Act 1998. This was only brought into operation from April 1st 1999, after the study had commenced and accordingly our research has not dealt with the use of such orders.

❏ The need for research

There are two principal reasons for undertaking research into the use of legal remedies to control anti-social behaviour.

First, many of the changes to the law have been justified on the assumption that the existing law is deficient or inadequate. A review of the literature on legal remedies for neighbour nuisance published in 1998 (Hunter *et al.*, 1998) concluded, however:

> "...*the critics of existing legal processes have not established the case that existing legal remedies are not working satisfactorily. Various specific problems have been alleged – delay, expense, difficulties of proof, judicial attitudes, enforcement – but the informational base of the criticisms is weak.*"

The report went on to recommend that future research attempt to establish an accurate picture of how the legal process is working in practice and that this should be organised around the various different remedies.

Secondly, underlying the calls for a strengthening of landlords' powers to contain and control the problem, is the belief that the problem can be tackled by ever increasing legislation. Whether such a belief is justified depends on an understanding of the nature of the problem. There has, however, been very little if any, systematic evaluation of the nature of the problem and the particular characteristics of households involved in incidences of neighbour nuisance. Despite this lack of information, popular perceptions have developed along with the use of the term 'anti-social behaviour' rather than 'neighbour nuisance'. The choice of the term 'anti-social behaviour' is significant since it conveys images which inform both the nature of the problem and possible remedies:

> "*Nuisance behaviour or neighbour disputes are much more benign terms than anti-social behaviour. The former suggests that such behaviour can be remedied in gentle and civilised ways whereas the latter suggests that the perpetrators are against or outside society, rejecting norms and values by their behaviours which marks them out as deviant and dangerous and in need of tough remedial action*" (Papps, 1998).

A cursory scrutiny of media coverage of the issue shows that the use of demonising stereotypes is indeed very prevalent. For example, a recent newspaper article was headlined "*Nightmare neighbours*" and described households involved in anti-social behaviour as: "*neighbours from hell*" and "*those whose behaviour is often so foul that describing them as animals would be to malign other species*" (*The Sheffield Star*, 25/11/99). In the same week *Inside Housing*, the journal for professional housing officers, carried an article which characterised households in the following terms:

> "*Challenging is too often used as the euphemism for the bigoted, bullying behaviour of ignorant, selfish and dangerous people. It is unforgivable and it*

should indeed be challenged…We should focus on the calculating, callous, selfish bully who causes trouble wherever he…or she happens to live" (*Inside Housing*, 19/11/99, p. 11).

Use of such emotive, negative, imagery certainly focusses on the *"deviant and dangerous"* and possibly serves as a justification for *"tough remedial action."* It also underlines the need for research which seeks to go behind the imagery and provide a more complex and insightful understanding of the issues surrounding anti-social behaviour.

❑ The nature of the research

The research was undertaken in a number of ways. First, a postal survey questionnaire was sent to two-thirds of all local authorities and two-thirds of all general needs registered social landlords with a stock of over 500 dwellings. Secondly, in-depth case studies were undertaken in five areas looking at two landlords in each area and their experiences of using legal remedies in their local court(s). Finally data on tenants' experience of legal remedies and the legal process was obtained through a series of interviews with both complainants and alleged perpetrators. In addition, a database of 67 individual cases of anti-social behaviour was compiled. Full details of the study methodology are provided in Appendix 1.

All the landlords surveyed and those in the case studies were in England. The law applicable to such landlords also applies in Wales and the conclusions apply equally. Different legal powers apply in Scotland. (See Atkinson *et al.*, 2000)

❑ The structure of this report

An interim report on the questionnaire data has already been published (Nixon *et al.*, 1999). This final report brings together all the research findings, although readers may at times be referred to the interim report for greater detail regarding the questionnaire data. This report contains thirteen further chapters:

- Chapter 2 examines the nature of the problem, in particular how anti-social behaviour is understood by landlords and who the perpetrators are.

- Chapter 3 explores issues around information collection by landlords, particularly the recording and monitoring of information.

- Chapter 4 examines the tenancy agreements and information given to tenants and used by landlords.

- Chapter 5 looks at the important role of multi-agency working.

- Chapter 6 examines the use of specialist units and officers to deal with anti-social behaviour.

- Chapter 7 looks at the decision to take legal action, and the work that is undertaken before such a decision can be taken.

- Chapter 8 moves on to the process of commencing legal action, and in particular the use of Notices of Seeking Possession and the collection of evidence.

- Chapter 9 then examines the use of the two main legal remedies: possession and injunction, taking into account landlords' views on the effectiveness of such action.

- Chapter 10 examines the whole process from the point of view of tenants, both complainants and defendants.

- Chapter 11 examines the limited evidence which emerged relating to the costs of legal action.

- Chapter 12 looks at the use of introductory and starter tenancies.

- Chapter 13 explores the use of exclusions and raises questions about where evicted tenants move on to.

- Chapter 14 draws some conclusions.

Appendix 1 provides information on the study methodology. Appendices 2 and 3 provide further information on the classification of the questionnaire data.

Chapter 2

The Nature of the Problem

There is no commonly agreed definition of what is meant by the terms 'neighbour nuisance', 'neighbour disputes' and 'anti-social behaviour.' A range of different definitions are in use, some focussing predominantly on criminal conduct, others taking a broader approach embracing a wide range of behaviours, (Hunter *et al.*, 1998, pp 2-3). The lack of a common definition reflects a lack of clarity about the precise nature and scope of the problem. Before considering the range of different legal remedies used by social landlords and the effectiveness of these remedies to deal with incidents of neighbour nuisance, it is useful to outline the parameters of the problem: what behaviours constitute anti-social behaviour and the characteristics of households involved in such behaviours.

❑ What constitutes anti-social behaviour?

Almost all officers interviewed had a common understanding of the range of behaviours that could constitute neighbour nuisance or anti-social behaviour. These behaviours formed a wide continuum from minor problems with dogs, children, untidy gardens and lifestyle clashes, through to serious noise problems, violent and criminal behaviour, racial harassment, intimidation and drug dealing. *"Anything which interferes with the peaceful enjoyment of the home and surrounding area,"* was one common catchall phrase. Officers also talked about behaviour, which made neighbours or the community, feel threatened, vulnerable, or uneasy. The behaviour could be directed at individuals or affect the wider neighbourhood.

While there was broad agreement about the general nature of the problem there were significant differences in how officers categorised individual incidents and at what stage they considered legal action appropriate. In particular, differences were noted in how officers dealt with minor but persistent problems as opposed to more serious incidents, which obviously transgressed wider social norms. The perceived 'reasonableness' of behaviour also varied with expectations and tolerance levels differing according to the location and type of estate or neighbourhood. Notwithstanding these differences, three main categories of anti-social behaviour were identified as warranting consideration for legal action.

- low level, but persistent behaviour;

- behaviour causing severe distress;

- behaviour having an adverse or potentially adverse effect on the wider neighbourhood.

In addition, cases were considered for legal action where many complaints had been made or where other (non-legal) means had failed to resolve the problem.

❏ The size of the problem

Due to deficiencies in landlords' recording, and monitoring systems, (see Chapter 3) no attempt could be made to measure the numerical incidence of the scale of the problem, but landlords were asked to give a subjective description of the perceived scale of the problem for their organisation. The majority of landlords reported that neighbour nuisance was a significant problem, with three-quarters of all landlords assessing it to be medium to large one.

Amongst local authorities perceptions of the size of the problem varied according to organisational type and size, with large, metropolitan authorities *eight times more likely* to think that they had a big or very big problem as compared to non-metropolitan authorities. Geographical differences in the perceived scale of the problem were also noted with authorities in the West Midlands, the North West and Yorkshire and Humberside most likely to perceive the problem to be a big or very big problem.

Chart 1: The regional distribution of LAs with a big or very big problem

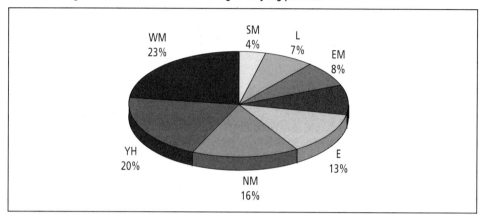

The patterns of regional variation in local authorities' assessment of the scale of anti-social behaviour was to some extent similar to the regional distribution of social housing in low demand as reported by the Social Exclusion Unit, Unpopular Housing Action Team (DETR, 1999). This finding confirms earlier work which found crime and anti-social behaviour to be the most commonly cited problems in areas of low demand housing (Cole *et al.*, 1999).

Chart 2: The regional distribution of RSLs with a big or very big problem

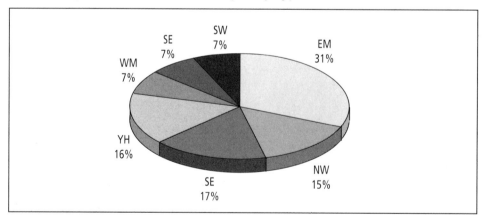

The regional distribution of registered social landlords who considered that they had a big or very big problem with anti-social behaviour was less clearly defined; as well as Northern based landlords some landlords operating in the South East and East Midlands also considered the problem to be a significant one.

■ Is the problem increasing?

Although it is impossible to assess the extent of the problem, or to gauge whether the problem is growing, there appears to have been an increase in legal action taken by landlords, with eight out of ten landlords stating that they had increased their use of legal remedies over the last five years. This finding could be interpreted as an indication of an increase in anti-social behaviour or at least an increase in the number of complaints made. Alternatively, the increase in legal action may simply reflect the fact that landlords are taking a more pro-active legal approach to the problem. Data from the case study landlords confirmed that the numbers of complaints were increasing, although caution was expressed by most officers in translating this increase into an equivalent increase in the incidence of serious anti-social behaviour which warranted legal action. Indeed some front line officers expressed the view that incidents of serious problems had not increased to any significant extent. Numerous reasons were given for the increase in complaints.

- There was a perception that there was greater intolerance amongst the population generally, which generated more minor complaints than previously.

- It was also felt that tenants had greater expectations of landlords, partly as a result of publicity created by the media and the high profile which this had generated.

- People were more likely to go to their landlord rather than try and sort the problem out themselves.

- Other reasons given for the reported increase in incidences referred to the wider symptoms of social exclusion and residualisation of social housing, combined with the impact of allocation policies which focus exclusively on housing need. For example, one front line officer commented:

  "Most of the people who are referred to us now have a support need for one reason or another, they're vulnerable in some way. So there's a chance that they will cause nuisance and if we're not made aware that there's a problem when we do take them on initially, we can't make sure that all the proper support networks are in place."

- Officers also thought some neighbourhoods were more susceptible than others to neighbour nuisance problems. Family estates, whether in more rural or urban environments, were singled out, as were mixed tenure sites and heavily populated neighbourhoods which included communal blocks of flats. A senior RSL officer commented on how newer households, invariably younger and from a more deprived and unsettled background, with existing social problems, moving into a more settled neighbourhood, could create problems.

"We are re-housing mainly deprived families, homeless families, people who have already got existing social problems, probably, and obviously that doesn't help because they're concentrated to a fairly large degree on the estates, and that doesn't help either."

It is also possible that the increase in complaints is due to improvements in landlords' method of recording complaints and subsequent action (see Chapter 3). Reports from the case study landlords indicated that where an organisation had made a strategic decision to give support and resources to deal with anti-social behaviour, officers had more confidence in tackling cases. This increased confidence amongst tenants that action would be taken, and therefore a belief that it would be more worth their while to report problems. This could also lead to a greater use of legal remedies.

❑ Who commits anti-social behaviour?

Officers' views about the types of households which were most likely to become involved in anti-social behaviour, highlighted the frequency with which people with support needs were the subject of complaints. Examples were given of people with mental health or drug problems or where there were problems associated with young people feeling that they had nothing to do. Defence lawyers also confirmed that a large percentage of their clients were vulnerable, often with mental health problems and many with community care needs. The prevalence of mental health problems in anti-social behaviour cases was also commented on by an experienced lawyer, who worked for nearly 40 housing associations, and spent 60 per cent of her time dealing with anti-social behaviour cases.

Evidence of vulnerabilities
The perception that households involved in anti-social behaviour had multiple problems was reinforced by the more detailed evidence obtained from the survey of 67 individual anti-social behaviour case files.

Very high levels of vulnerability or disadvantage were recorded, with two-thirds of defendants (67 per cent) described in the files as having a particular problem or special needs. It should be noted that not all case files contained information about the particular characteristics of households, so it is possible that the proportion of people with vulnerabilities might be even larger than that recorded in the sample.

Table 1: Type of vulnerability recorded on file[1]

Type of vulnerability	No.	%
Physical or sexual abuse	12	18%
Mental disability	12	18%
Out of control children	10	15%
Drugs problem	8	12%
Alcohol problem	7	11%
Physical disability	6	9%

Given the high incidence of substance abuse and out of control children within the sample it is not perhaps surprising that a relatively high incidence of criminal activities was also noted on file, with just over a quarter of households reported as having previous convictions for criminal offences including theft, handling stolen goods, and drug related offences. Where criminal activity had been noted it was not always the cause of the initial complaint.

Household composition and source of income

Just under two-thirds of households (61 per cent) included children, with 36 per cent consisting of sole parents and 25 per cent of two parent families. Very high levels of poverty and benefit dependency were found in the sample. Only three households were stated to be in employment, with the remaining 92 per cent of households dependant on welfare benefits.

Given the evidence of high levels of poverty it is interesting to note that the incidence of rent arrears was not found to be any greater than in the general

---

1. Many defendants were recorded as having more than one of the problems listed and therefore the percentages do not add up to 100 per cent.

population of social housing tenants (DoE, 1994), with only four out of ten households (40 per cent) reported as having rent arrears.

Length of tenancy

The date of the commencement of the tenancy for households in the sample ranged from over 35 years to less than one year. There was no evidence to suggest that problems were more likely to occur in new tenancies since the majority of households (54 per cent) had been tenants since 1994, i.e. for at least four years with less than eight (12 per cent) households having held tenancies for less than two years duration. This finding suggests that introductory or starter tenancies (see Chapter 12), may only have a limited effect in preventing anti-social behaviour.

❏ The nature of the complaints

The defendant survey showed that in some cases complaints had been received over a long period of time with the earliest complaint on file recorded over 14 years ago in 1985. However, in the majority of cases (35), complaints had been made more recently with 58 per cent of first complaints having occurred over the last two years. In three-quarters of cases more than one complaint was recorded on file and in one extreme example over 28 different complaints were recorded. Interestingly, in four cases no complaint was formally recorded on file. In these cases, possession action was initiated directly by the landlord generally in response to previous criminal convictions, which did not appear to have given rise to complaints from neighbours. Table 2 provides information about the type of behaviours complained about.

Most commonly, complaints focussed on behaviours involving verbal abuse and noise, with half of all complaints making reference to these problems. Problems arising as a result of violence and unruly children accounted for a further third of complaints. The in-depth interviews with complainants confirmed that initial complaints most commonly related to noise nuisance with the problems subsequently escalating to incorporate abuse, harassment and even physical assault. Previous studies have highlighted the problems of the rising incidence of crime and disorder on social housing estates with landlords expressing concern about the increase in drug abuse, housebreaking, and vandalism. Government responses have also tended to focus on the problem of criminal activity (Papps, 1998). Analysis of the

Table 2: Categories of complaint recorded on file[2]

Complaint	No.	%
Verbal abuse	37	55%
Noise	37	55%
Violence	23	34%
Unruly children	22	33%
Drink/drugs	19	28%
Litter/rubbish	13	19%
Criminal convictions	11	16%
Gardens	8	12%
Dogs/pets	7	10%
Racial harassment	5	8%

complaints on file suggests that criminal activity is in fact a minority problem. Only 16 per cent of initial complaints concern criminal activity such as arson, drug abuse, and burglary, with a further 8 per cent of complaints concerning racial harassment.

❏ Summary

The problem of neighbour nuisance and anti-social behaviour is difficult to classify and impossible to quantify. It is clearly a dynamic phenomenon, involving a broad range of disruptive behaviours, which in more serious cases can escalate from noise nuisance through to abuse and even physical attacks. Households involved in anti-social behaviour were predominantly characterised as having high levels of vulnerability, including mental health problems and other disabilities. Most defendants were dependent on state benefits of some kind. These findings are directly relevant to future policy development. If landlords are to implement effective strategies to deal with anti-social behaviour, the complex and dynamic nature of the problem should not be underestimated.

---

2. In many cases more than one complaint was specified on the file thus the percentages recorded do not add up to 100 per cent.

CHAPTER 3

RECORDING AND MONITORING

Record keeping and information collection are an essential component in monitoring the success or otherwise of any policy. The survey findings highlighted the difficulties many landlords experienced gathering accurate information relating to the scale of the problem and the methods used to deal with it. A third of local authorities (34 per cent) and over a half of registered social landlords (56 per cent) failed to keep records of the number of complaints received, with only a minority of landlords able to provide detailed data on the progress of individual cases. In 1996/97 less than a quarter of landlords (16 per cent RSLs and 22 per cent LAs) could provide detailed data on individual cases. There was some evidence that improvement in monitoring of cases were taking place since in 1997/98, 26 per cent of registered social landlords and 41 per cent of local authorities were able to provide this data. Scrutiny of defendant case files, however, confirmed that information about individual cases was frequently not adequately recorded or monitored. In a number of files it was impossible to identify exactly what action had been taken, what the current position was and if the case had been resolved.

❏ Reasons for the failure to record and monitor complaints

Numerous reasons were given as to why landlords did not have comprehensive monitoring systems.

Registered social landlords
Many registered social landlords had very poor or non-existent systems, either manual or computerised. Even where computerised systems were used they were often not set up to record anti-social behaviour incidents separately

from rent or other issues, and they did not always record the serving of Notices of Seeking Possession (NSPs) separately from other forms of legal action. There were also examples of landlords combining rent arrears and anti-social behaviour cases in the monitoring of cases involving legal action. For some registered social landlords the lack of monitoring was attributed to the small size of the organisation or because the problem was perceived to be too small to monitor. On the other hand, some of the larger landlords had a particular problem due to a decentralised structure covering a wide geographical area which resulted in difficulties in aggregating data from area offices, or 'business units':

> *"There is not a central overview, so for example, we don't, at head office, have a data base with all this information for the association as a whole across its six areas. It's a bit of a gap. In the areas, they will have a good idea, but they would probably have to refer to files and a bit of work before they could come up with some figures. In terms of monitoring cases on a day to day basis, yes, that does happen…supervision and so on, and we do keep abreast of what the housing officers are doing."*

A few landlords had a manual system with a separate complaints file from the tenancy file. Some organisations used special stationery for the recording of complaints which was then stored in a separate complaints' file. Often data was collated for monthly or quarterly reports, but these figures were not compiled on an annual basis, thus making year by year comparisons difficult. Three organisations only logged complaints on individual tenancy files with no method of monitoring the total number of complaints received or the action taken to deal with different categories of complaints. On the whole, registered social landlords were less organised in this area than local authorities.

One front line officer regretted that her organisation did not make area statistics available to other areas and estates, as it would be helpful to see how they compared and how others were trying to resolve the situation, as well as help reduce the sense of isolation amongst officers scattered over a wide area.

> *"It can be a source of information. If I'm aware that somebody's taken action against a perpetrator for x, and if I have similar problem then I can talk to that officer. It's useful to get the overall picture, just to get a feel of what's happening in the area on the estates that we manage. Just like where you fit into the bigger picture."*

Local authorities

Although local authorities were more likely than registered social landlords to have recording systems, many acknowledged that their recording systems were poor, with some also attributing lack of monitoring on their small size, which precluded the necessity for such sophistication. Officers reported that information tended to be held 'in the head' and by talking with other officers.

> *"Because we deal with so few, it isn't a growing problem that we have to monitor those. We know the individual case…If it got to such a stage where it was becoming an overriding problem in terms of the work load for housing officers, in terms of the amount of work we're having to deal on court action, on legal notices, then we'd review the whole exercise."*

A few authorities stated compulsory competitive tendering provisions had restricted their ability to monitor, which the researchers speculated to mean that the commercial environment in which the contractors were operating made the information too sensitive.

Data from the case study landlords confirmed the lack of a consistent approach to recording and monitoring. Commonly, a range of rather idiosyncratic processes were employed at the initial complaint stage, which more often than not were not linked to the eventual outcome, nor was it easy to retrieve information about how particular problems were resolved, if they did not end in eviction. As one front line officer commented, *"Everyone has their own way of doing things."* Even where an organisation had some kind of system, it was acknowledged that in practice adherence to it could be inconsistent. A local authority senior officer admitted: *"The truth is, because our monitoring system has been so weak it's very hard to count [the number of NSPs served] reliably…"*

One of the reasons given for the difficulties in recording cases concerned the complexity of anti-social behaviour cases.

> *"I think the monitoring that we do, the monitoring forms and the admin. involved with dealing with anti-social behaviour is very cumbersome and it suits if you've got two neighbours in a dispute over a dog barking…it fits in neatly with the paperwork and the monitoring forms…But if you've got something quite complex or ongoing it doesn't fit in very well with the monitoring."*

Scrutiny of the defendant case files and interviews with tenants confirmed that anti-social behaviour cases tend not to be straightforward and linear.

Reliable recording processes need to take into account the fact that cases are dynamic and complex.

There was awareness amongst most of the case study landlords that recording and information systems needed to be improved and many officers commented that it would be beneficial to be able to follow the progress of cases in order to discover how serious complaints were resolved, and if there were patterns emerging.

A few organisations were in the process of redesigning organisational structures and explicit systems to improve the current situation. An example was given by a senior local authority officer of an old system, about to be redesigned:

> *"It was just nonsense really. There wasn't any clarity about whether you put in cases for that particular month or whether you put in all the live cases and people were doing different things. And the different categories were just plucked out of the air anyway. It was like writing an essay without a plan. And it's just so that you can have a chart. And it proved very little. It probably gave us a total number of cases up to a point but nothing more than that. People did not take it seriously. It didn't figure in any performance league tables either. If people aren't held to account for their information they don't care about it."*

The recent draft Housing Corporation performance standards on the development of long-term strategies for dealing with anti-social behaviour focusses attention even more greatly on this deficit (Housing Corporation, 1999). But clear guidance will be needed, as one registered social landlord pointed out:

> *"We'd have to have to have very clear guidance from [the Housing Corporation] in the first place about what they expected us to record, because if they wanted us to record every single time that somebody phoned up to complain about their neighbour, then you'd spend half your life doing it."*

Specialist units

Where there was either a specialist unit or officer, then the detailed recording and monitoring improved once the case had been referred to them. Local offices often held their own records of the complaints and how they had been dealt with up to referral to the specialist officers. Computers could provide a reliable system, but were not necessarily seen as the only tool for improvement. A specialist officer in a medium sized local authority had developed his own manual system which was quite adequate for the task and was felt to provide some safeguards over data protection inherent in computerised records.

❑ Summary

Although the research findings illustrate the many difficulties landlords experienced in accurately monitoring the progress of cases there were also examples of good practice, which need to be built upon.

CHAPTER 4

INFORMATION FOR TENANTS/ TENANCY AGREEMENTS

Following the 1996 Housing Act an increasing number of landlords have inserted specific clauses relating to nuisance behaviour into their tenancy agreements. The use of such clauses can be important in both obtaining possession and injunctions (see Hunter, 2000). We sought to examine how far landlords sought to encourage good behaviour through the use of such clauses and through the provision of information to tenants and sign-up procedures.

❏ Terms of the tenancy

Landlords were asked in the survey to provide information about their tenancy agreements and whether they had been revised since the 1996 Housing Act. Three-quarters of all landlords (74 per cent) had done so. We also asked them to enclose copies of their tenancy agreements and over half did so. Scrutiny of these tenancy agreements showed the diversity of clauses on nuisance behaviour, which could be categorised into three types (greater detail is provided in Section 4 of the Interim Report):

- The very general clause on nuisance behaviour.
- The longer clause which covers a wider range of behaviour and specifically deals with harassment.
- Those which gave examples of the types of behaviour excluded and defined what they meant in more exacting terms.

Some survey respondents commented that they felt that it was better to have a more generalised clause rather than one which was too specific since, *"it avoids potential behaviour not being contrary"* to the agreement. This would then be supplemented by examples of behaviour, which according to one respondent were, *"not part of the agreement."* One respondent, however, stated exactly the opposite, i.e. that it was better to have specific clauses rather than something too general. No clear view on this emerged from the case studies, although two landlords expressed the view that tightening up of the words in the tenancy agreement had actually made a positive difference to the decisions made in the court.

❏ Information given to tenants

Most landlords stated that they paid special attention to the sections on anti-social behaviour in tenancy agreements when signing-up new tenants. This action was also seen to be helpful if court action became necessary. One senior local authority officer explained:

> *"As far as people who are likely subsequently to breach the agreement the thing that should be happening at the lettings interview is that a very clear marker is being laid down about the standard of behaviour that is expected of them, and it should be possible in terms of our subsequent legal actions for an officer who has let a property out to be able to say very clearly that they followed our lettings procedures and that they have been careful in bringing the issues of standards of behaviour to the attention of a tenant who has subsequently breached. So it should be helpful in terms of future legal action."*

However, the emphasis given at the sign-up stage was not solely to warn potential 'trouble-makers', but also to reassure the majority of tenants that the landlord would be taking action to ensure their quiet enjoyment of their home, and protecting them from others. Even though every landlord made great effort at sign-up stage to emphasise the terms of the agreement, with one saying that they had a two-hour sign-up process, there are concerns about how much is actually understood by some tenants.

> *"...there are still a lot of people who cannot read and write properly and who nod in the right places and give you the impression that they've understood, when really they haven't, and there's a bit of a lesson there I think for everyone."*

Most of the complainants interviewed had been tenants for many years and had signed 'old' tenancy agreements issued prior to the Housing Act 1996 amendments had been introduced. Of the seven tenant complainants, five stated that prior to experiencing disruptive behaviour from their neighbours they had not been aware of the landlord's policy and procedures on anti-social behaviour. Although all the tenants had signed tenancy agreements and some had been issued with additional information, the majority were unaware of their landlord's policy on neighbour nuisance. As one couple in their late 50s explained, *"Well actually we didn't really read it did we?"* Another couple of tenants stated that prior to directly experiencing neighbour nuisance, *"we didn't know nothing"* about the landlord's neighbour nuisance policies and procedures. The owner-occupiers interviewed also stated that the landlord who owned the adjoining property had not given them any information about the organisation's neighbour nuisance policies when they moved into the area.

Ways of informing existing tenants of changes to the terms of the tenancy are done through occasional newsletters and leaflets which can be picked up at the housing office. The newsletter would also often be used to reinforce the message that the landlord would take action in anti-social behaviour cases and publicise actions that had been taken. Newsletters were also used to publicise the development and changes in the landlord's policies and procedures relating to action on anti-social behaviour. Leaflets were also often used, sometimes sent to all tenants, and sometimes available upon request. Tenants' committees were also mentioned as fora where information about the landlord's approach was disseminated. In most cases there would appear to be little formal involvement from tenants in the formulation of the policy changes, but housing officers did appear to feel that these sort of changes had the full support of the majority of tenants. For instance, this officer from a registered social landlord operating in the North:

> *"We sent out key areas of where we've made big changes [to our policies] and one of those areas was in terms of anti-social behaviour. That went to all tenants and we asked them to give their views and whether they supported us...a lot of responses coming from our tenants was we're glad you're doing this, please get tough on anti-social tenants, and also make sure that when you're choosing your tenants you're putting the right ones in, in the first place."*

❏ Summary

Generally, the changes to tenancy agreements, stimulated by the 1996 Housing Act, were seen by landlords to have made a positive contribution in preventing anti-social behaviour. Officers thought that methods of informing tenants of changes to their tenancy agreement were very effective. However, interviews with tenants raised some doubts over the extent to which tenancy agreements were actually read or understood by tenants.

CHAPTER 5

MULTI-AGENCY WORKING

It is now recognised that the development of effective strategies to prevent and deal with nuisance behaviours requires landlords to adopt a multi-agency approach with input from a range of agencies and local government departments (CIH, 1998, p 3). The need to develop nuisance strategy partnerships was generally recognised amongst the case study organisations, with social services and the police being the two principal agencies involved in such partnerships. Some of the case study landlords had developed more formal, partnerships with the police and other local agencies through the use of Safer Estates Agreements.

In principle, all the case study landlords said they had a commitment to develop effective multi-agency partnerships. Two landlords stated they would always involve social services and the police in cases where legal action was being considered, often calling a case conference to share information and if possible to devise an agreed strategy to prevent the issuing of a Notice of Seeking Possession (NSP). In one area, a service level agreement pilot project, involving the police, local social landlords and others, was being set up to develop joint policies to deal with anti-social behaviour. In another area, preventative work was being undertaken with drug and alcohol agencies with an agreed protocol for establishing care management packages in the event of a household being evicted. A further example of innovation was found in a project developed by the probation service in conjunction with local housing organisations and other agencies, to provide support in cases involving, for example, sex offenders, drug and mental health problems. This initiative was running in parallel with a Safer Estates Agreement involving the police.

Another possible partner organisation are environmental health departments, which have powers to deal with nuisances, particularly noise. Interestingly only one case study organisation (a local authority) regularly referred noise nuisance cases to its environmental health department for action. Some landlords, in particular two registered social landlords, had experienced problems with trying to engage with the their local environmental health department, which, for budgetary reasons, appeared reluctant to take any responsibility for noise nuisance cases.

Landlords were aware of the potential benefits of joint working and stated that the sharing of information between agencies about what they could and could not do and identifying the problems from their different perspectives, contributed to helping build better communication and more effective partnerships. However, for most landlords, in practice, joint working was often fraught with difficulties and was dependant on partners being prepared to understand and negotiate around different organisational cultures with different agendas and different budget limitations,

> *"Certainly multi-agency working…is…becoming even more important than it used to be and there's difficulties around that,…because as a housing department we're not viewed as necessarily equipped to need to know certain information about families that are living in the community. There's still this view that we are concerned with the bricks and mortar and we're not really concerned with anything else and that causes problems when we're the first to find out."*

❏ Working with social services

Although partnerships with social services departments were seen to be an essential part of a multi-agency approach, the case study landlords had, almost without exception, experienced difficulties in developing joint working practices with social services. Housing officers' criticisms of local social service departments focussed on their lack of co-operation, with a reluctance to get involved in individual cases unless there was a self-referral or legal action for possession had been commenced. Commonly, officers felt frustrated at the lack of support forthcoming from social services, these views were echoed in the comments provided in the survey.

> *"It seems the only way you can actually get the social services, mental health workers and the doctors…to sit up and take notice, [is] to get them so wound up, that [they think]: 'how dare somebody serve a notice on my client, because, don't they realise this person's ill', and you think: 'Well, perhaps if you'd been paying more attention to your client in the first place, and giving them the support they needed, the illness wouldn't have got that bad that we've been in the position to have to serve a notice'."*

In response to these difficulties, it was not uncommon for possession action to be initiated in order to gain a response from social services.

> *"There is a reluctance of the social services to become involved in nuisance cases. To a certain extent the housing department is left to take inappropriate action…, but sometimes we have to do it to actually bring social services on board."*

It was also noted that there could be a conflict of interests between social services and housing departments. On occasions this had resulted in differing views being expressed in court – social services arguing for retention of the home, and the housing department determined to follow through with an eviction. Concern was also expressed by housing officers that even in the event of an eviction involving children or other vulnerable groups, there was a lack of support from social service departments.

❏ Working with the police

Joint working between landlords and the police was seen as important at various points in the life cycle of potential and actual anti-social behaviour problems, through pro-active, preventative and strategic development, as well as in helping to obtain the necessary evidence for a court case. Information sharing frequently formed the basis of landlords' partnerships with the police and when it worked properly was a two-way process assisting both the landlord and the police. Information from landlords may assist the police in bringing a criminal prosecution, which may be one way of dealing with a particular problem. On the other hand, police information concerning criminal convictions may be used by landlords as a ground for possession.

Formal information sharing protocols
Data from the survey and from the case study areas showed that landlords had put considerable effort into developing good relationships with the police. Most landlords had some form of information exchange protocol with more formalised partnerships in the process of being developed as a result of Safer Estates initiatives and through the provisions of the Crime and Disorder Act 1998. The survey findings showed that nearly three-quarters of local authorities (71 per cent) and half of all registered social landlords had an agreed information exchange protocol with the police, but as Chart 3 shows for registered social landlords in particular, there were strong regional differences in the distribution of formal protocols. For example, while 82 per cent of those in Yorkshire and Humberside had such agreements, only 17 per cent of registered social landlords in the East region had a formal protocol.

Chart 3: Proportion of landlords who have an information sharing protocol with the police – by region

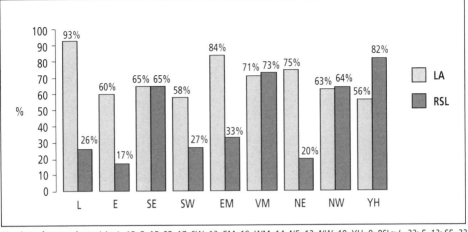

Number of respondents: *LAs: L=15; E=15; SE=17; SW=12; EM=19; WM=14; NE=12; NW=19; YH=9; RSLs: L=23; E=12; SE=23; SW=11; EM=3; WM=15; NE=5; NW=11; YH=11*

In some areas, formal partnerships under the 1998 Crime and Disorder Act (CDA) provisions were beginning to be implemented, with others in the process of development. Although such partnerships should in theory include all social landlords operating within an area, in practice registered social landlords often seemed to be excluded from the development of the partnership. There was also some evidence to suggest that there was lack of understanding amongst some police officers about the role of registered social landlords and their obligations to co-operate with them.

In addition to formal information sharing protocols, Safer Estate Agreements were in the process of being developed in many areas. Typically, such agreements adopt a three-prong approach, for example:

- *"To co-operate in the development of policies to improve the effectiveness of both the police and housing departments in tackling the problems of crime and harassment on council estates.*
- *To pursue all available legal remedies through both the criminal and civil courts with a view to modifying the behaviour of offending individuals and effecting a lasting solution.*
- *To increase the confidence of residents in the ability of the police and local authorities to combat these problems and to encourage their support in combating crime and harassment."*

Source: Safer Estates Partnership between Social Landlord and Staffordshire Police, 1994

Many registered social landlords owned property located across a number of local authority and police areas. This geographical spread meant that they invariably found themselves dealing with a range of different arrangements and expectations. This highlighted the acutely variable nature of responses, even where partnerships had been established under the CDA. One case study solicitor spoke about a CID officer telling them they could, *"stuff the Safer Estates Agreement."* Nevertheless, there were localised examples of good working relationships, at both an informal and formal level.

> *"...at its best, we've got direct dial numbers of all the local community policemen and their sergeants and the CID office and we can ring them up and say, 'Oh it's X from X, I found this out', very informal, but very regular basis...we can ring each other with information. And also in terms of formally giving information, they have attended, they have given us statements for us to use in court and have been fine about that. In other areas, you can ring the police to find out some information, if we know they've been called out, and you're lucky if you get your phone call returned. Or they'll hide behind 'that's data protection, I can't tell you that', not even on an informal basis. It varies, I mean we've done our best to develop the relationships but it doesn't always happen."*

Landlords' experience of information exchange systems

Despite the prevalence of formal protocols, on the ground their effect was found to be very variable, and often needed the active support of key officers. Housing officers tended to favour the use of more informal arrangements, which provided useful and readily accessible information. Indeed developing successful partnerships with the police was, perhaps more than with other organisations, seen as being dependent on the commitment and character of individual officers in building up good relationships at the local level. Many of the difficulties of joint working, cited by both housing officers and their lawyers, revolved around the frustrating differences between formal and informal arrangements. This was reflected through the more amenable and constructive relationships being developed at the local beat level compared with the obstacles perceived to arise from the rigid hierarchies operating in the police force.

For a few organisations it appeared impossible to overcome such difficulties and establish good local relationships and this caused much frustration.

> *"I think the police could play a crucial, very important role. But...all too often it tends to come down to the relationship that the housing officer has with the beat officer in the passing of information. Some beat officers are very good and they will gladly exchange information because they've built up a trust with the*

housing officer. Other beat officers tend to be strictly by-the-rule people where they'll say, 'well, I'm sorry but, you know, we're not allowed to give any information to you but can you give us any?'…we get that a lot."

If these difficulties are to be overcome the corporate structures need to be strengthened so that relationships are not based on the personal interaction.

Data protection

Much frustration was expressed about the huge inconsistency of approach and a lack of understanding of the provisions of the Data Protection Act, that could be experienced between different divisions and forces:

"Officers don't know what their obligations for disclosure are, and they don't know what they are allowed to say, and so they'll tell you virtually anything privately, but then qualify it with a, 'well you can't rely on that'. I actually find that one police force has differences of policy between police stations which are about two miles apart."

Perhaps on occasions housing officers had too great an expectation of what the police could disclose, since under the Data Protection Act it must be directly relevant to action the housing officer could take.

"They only tell us what they think we ought to know or what we need to know. So as an example, if we said to them, 'Can you confirm whether or not you have ever been called to one of our addresses, in relation to anti-social behaviour?', they might say, 'Yes, we've been out there four times, persons have been cautioned'. But they might not necessarily tell us that the tenant has been charged with shoplifting [outside the area]".

Understanding landlords' powers

There were also concerns amongst some landlords that the police lacked knowledge and information about landlords' powers. One officer thought that the police overestimated the powers of landlords and used this as a reason for abdicating responsibility for taking action. Examples were given of the police looking to public sector landlords to take action, through the use of injunctions and possession action in order to help them bring to an end criminal behaviour of a persistent offender, e.g. stealing cars on the estate. Although some examples were given of joint training initiatives these were the exception rather than the rule, but could be utilised to provide a better understanding.

This appeared particularly true for the successful enforcement of injunctions, where it was felt that it was vital to have a good relationship with the local police. One private solicitor compared trying to get police to co-operate to, *"trying to knit fog."*

Evidence in court

Being able to use police evidence in court was seen by lawyers as extremely beneficial but could be very hard to come by. A frustrated front line housing officer also commented on how useful police evidence could be but how difficult it was to obtain:

> *"If I went to court for instance with [our solicitor] I'd like to go in with a list of how many times the police were called out to the property. You can't have it…"*

Here again the lines were drawn between formal and informal knowledge, as was illustrated by one housing officer:

> *"We get a very good relationship from the police on the estate, so informally it can be just to pick up a phone and say, 'Look, I've got a problem with such and such', and they can look on the computer and, 'Oh well, they've got their partner living there now who's a known drug dealer. I'll go round and have a word'. That's very informal."*

Such a good relationship was not however, apparent when seeking formal evidence:

> *"The problems arise…when legal action is required and then you have to go down the official channels…You have to sign all the necessary documents and get all the necessary authorisation and it takes a very long time and it does drag out the process. That's where you hit your first obstacle."*

Landlords reported that the willingness of the police to provide formal evidence differed tremendously from one area to another, with one police area being very helpful with formal statements for use in court, but in other areas a variety of excuses were used as to why they could not do this. A senior housing officer commented:

> *"…when we write to the police and ask them for a chronological list of incidents on that property we find there is a great time delay in getting evidence, and often the police are ignorant in terms of what they can supply and what they can't, as are [we]…"*

Two organisations, both registered social landlords, even reported that they had been asked for payment from the police for giving evidence in court, which did not help the relationship between them, and another had to subpoena officers in order to ensure their attendance at the court hearing.

Some landlords were concerned by difficulties in obtaining information from the police about criminal offences, which may constitute a ground for possession. Providing the information after a court conviction might be too late for the landlord to take action for possession. Examples were given of where the police had simply forgotten to inform the housing organisation. Yet with another organisation (a local authority) this sort of information was provided with little difficulty under their local protocol.

Working together

Other ways that housing officers and the police had found to work together included high profile, joint patrols on estates. One organisation's joint patrols issued written undertakings or cautions if behaviour was likely to be in breach of the tenancy agreement, for instance to the parents of an unruly child. Although these undertakings were not legal documents, it was felt they were effective as a warning. Other organisations had set up joint interviewing of perpetrators with the police providing information about the provisions of the Protection from Harassment Act 1997. Such initiatives were seen as providing a more effective deterrent than if warnings were given solely by housing officers.

> "[We have] an extremely good working relationship with the local community sergeant and we don't let data protection bog us down too much. We're aware that there are problems in terms of sharing information but there's things that we can do. One way of getting round that sometimes is to have joint interviews…Again, in terms of a deterrent, it's quite successful as well."

❑ Summary

The research findings indicate that although considerable resources have been put into developing multi-agency partnerships, principally involving the police and social landlords, in practice such partnerships were fraught with problems. In particular, relationships with social service departments were singled out for criticism. Given households involved in anti-social behaviour are likely to have multiple problems there is clearly an urgent need for social landlords and social service departments to develop better relationships. Overall, it was recognised that there were many difficulties to overcome, in order to achieve more fruitful partnership working. Issues that required addressing included the problems arising from different organisational cultures, agendas, and lack of understood and agreed communication channels. Notwithstanding these difficulties many landlords were optimistic that improvements would be realised as protocols and relationships became more established.

CHAPTER 6

SPECIALIST UNITS

The use of specialist units and officers whose work is primarily, if not entirely, devoted to implementing the organisation's anti-social behaviour policy is becoming more common. Dedicated officers working alongside strengthened organisational policy and support, say something about the organisation's commitment and direction of limited resources to dealing with problems that otherwise go unreported and unchecked, but cause misery and distress for many parties. The specialist unit or officer can have a range of roles within the process from facilitating multi-agency working, to gathering evidence and supporting witnesses, through to providing evidence in court.

❑ Models of provision

Three landlords in our case studies operated, or had access to, specialist support of some kind. The different types of provision represented three models of specialist support appropriate for different organisations, with different sizes of stock and different perceptions of the scale of the problem.

- **Model 1** – A neighbour nuisance unit, employing a team of specialist and legal staff to co-ordinate action on all aspects of neighbour disputes.
- **Model 2** – An individual specialist officer working with housing and legal officers to assist and advise on neighbour nuisance cases.
- **Model 3** – Use of an external agency to act as an agent for the landlord providing guidance on appropriate action, including supporting witnesses and assisting in the preparation of legal action.

The examples of each of the three models provided by the case study landlords indicated how schemes could be developed to work efficiently in particular circumstances. A large specialist unit had been set up in November

1995 by a large metropolitan landlord with tens of thousands of stock. It comprised of two specialist, dedicated solicitors, eight nuisance response officers, three administrative staff (which was about to increase) and a team leader.

A smaller authority, with only 7,000 stock, managed quite comfortably with one specialist tenancy enforcement officer (TEO). This officer, who had developed a tough reputation in order to be effective, operated within the legal section, but was responsible to the housing department. The TEO also worked with a project team, which included a police liaison officer, an in-house solicitor, as well as housing officers. This team discussed cases on a fortnightly basis.

Both the above models were set up following a review of policy and strategy and resulted in direct improvements in the relationship between housing officers and the organisation's legal department. Both schemes primarily provided a comprehensive evidence collection and witness support services, but also undertook training and gave support to front line housing officers.

The only equivalent specialist support service found amongst the case study registered social landlords was the Tenancy Enforcement Support Team (TEST). TEST, was set up as a small independent company in 1997, by seven registered social landlords in South London with the aim of tackling anti-social behaviour. TEST officers see themselves as, 'professional laymen', taking referrals from landlords for a 'cost-effective' flat fee per case regardless of how long they keep the case open, and what means are used to deal with it. An out of hours service is provided with the team prepared to investigate incidents between 7:30 p.m. to 2:30 a.m., 365 days a year. With only one case worker, one administrator and two part-time case workers for night time duty, they establish the facts from what they regard to be a more independent and possibly more objective perspective, weeding out non-genuine complainants, trying to resolve cases and providing evidence. Although currently TEST does not provided a legal service, they do give some advice to clients about the appropriateness of taking legal action, as well as when to serve a Notice of Seeking Possession.

❏ Benefits of specialism

Perhaps the most important benefit of specialist units/officers was the increased support and confidence that they gave front line housing officers in tackling problems of anti-social behaviour, along with the increased public profile that was given to the organisation. As a consequence of the increased confidence, skills and experience gained by housing officers there was likely to be an increase in trust from tenants in the ability and determination of their landlord in tackling difficult cases, thereby increasing the likelihood that tenants would be prepared to come forward and act as witnesses at the final court hearing. A senior officer in the specialist unit explained:

> *"The most significant success of the service has been the engagement of witnesses. Either directly ourselves or through the area housing teams, with training, support and giving of confidence to the area housing teams. We did find very very quickly that there is a current housing management mythology that you can't get witnesses. We found that witnesses need to know that their concerns would be taken seriously, that they would be listened to, that they'd be heard. If all those things were in place then witnesses would be engaged and if they could see the process that we had available to us to protect them, securing the orders of the court, in some very very few cases providing personal protection, that they would work with us and that they would see the sense of it."*

This was also recognised by their legal department.

> *"I think that fundamentally housing officers have found dealing with anti-social behaviour, nuisance complaints, a real bind, and when you don't like something you don't deal with it well. You can't change it overnight, it was a process of gradual education, confidence building, being available to baby-sit. Once they began to understand there's a reason why we have these procedures, because they work, they were confident to take on the complaints, speak to people in the way that people had confidence in. It became clear to the public that they were dealing with somebody that knew how to deal with the issue they were bringing forward..."*

Not only were specialist officers able to provide support to witnesses, they also had expertise in drawing up formal statements, and giving evidence directly to the court. Furthermore, their expertise and experience enabled them to assess cases and determine the most appropriate form of action.

Interviews with complainants confirmed the benefits of employing specialist officers. Almost without exception, they felt such officers provided them with greater support than they had received from the front line officers (see Chapter 10).

❑ Views of those without specialists

The type of responses by those organisations who did not have a specialist unit or specialist officers depended primarily on their size and whether they were a local authority or a registered social landlords. Many local authorities without units were either having discussions about the possibility, or were reviewing the situation. The wider remit of the Crime and Disorder Act was often cited as being a very good reason for providing a more specialist service for housing officers.

One senior local authority officer summed up the perceived advantages of a unit in the following way:

> "...focus, co-ordination and having legal advice on tap. It'll tackle some of the resources you use as well because its team does nothing else and it can prioritise the different harassment and anti-social behaviour cases. It can focus the resources round the borough appropriately..."

Registered social landlords also expressed the view that the provision of specialist support services would be valuable, however, many also felt that they would experience particular difficulties in trying to emulate this service, either because they were too small, or because they had offices spread throughout the country, making it impractical. Where a local authority specialist unit was in the vicinity, many registered social landlords thought it could be beneficial to be able to buy into its services, and discussions around this possibility were being held in one of the case study areas. The potential benefits of buying in specialist support focussed on reducing costs and passing on experience. It was also considered that access to a specialist service might reduce inconsistencies in approach currently taken by housing officers as well as reducing the sense of isolation when trying to undertake this kind of work. In addition, it was recognised that access to some of these services would also off-load work which greatly impinged on the huge variety of housing officers' day to day work.

There were only a few negative responses to the idea of specialist units or officers. One private solicitor thought that their current service would be much cheaper and more efficient than one provided through a local authority specialist unit. A front line officer expressed concern that using a service such as TEST would result in the officer's loss of control of the situation. She explained:

"Personally, I think that you'd lose grip of what was going on if someone else was doing the evidence gathering for you. If you were still going to remain the lead officer I think you should have direct involvement."

One further reservation was noted, with a senior officer stating that specialist units might reinforce the idea that social sector tenants needed to have their own police force because of the sort of people they were, and therefore the provision of such units contributed to the negative image of social housing and its tenants.

❑ Summary

Where a specialist service had been provided landlords stated that they had been crucial in improving the organisation's efficiency in dealing with the problems surrounding anti-social behaviour. Where no specialist service was available, landlords and their solicitors stated they would have liked to have access to such a service, either through replication or through access to other units. They were seen as contributing towards relieving housing officers from some of the more time consuming and specialist work as well as providing a more professional and committed service.

The degree to which this was seen as useful, and the level at which these specialisms were deemed appropriate depended, however, on the size of the organisation, with small organisations having to balance the perceived extent of the problem against the resources available to them.

CHAPTER 7

STRATEGIES TO AVOID LEGAL ACTION

The survey showed that for all landlords most complaints were dealt with without recourse to legal action. The research sought to establish what strategies landlords employed to avoid legal action and why some cases were resolved without the necessity of legal action whilst others were not.

Chart 4 shows the average number of complaints received by landlords in the period 1997/98 and the proportion of these complaints which, resulted in a Notice of Seeking Possession (NSP) being served. Amongst local authorities, on average 35 complaints had been made per 1,000 tenancies, with only one in every fifty complaints leading to a NSP being served. In contrast, registered social landlords reported far fewer recorded complaints, only 15 complaints per 1,000 tenancies being recorded but a higher proportion of complaints resulted in the service of a NSP. Taking into account these differences, in practice, both landlords served a similar number of NSPs per 1,000 tenancies.

This finding suggests that for most organisations legal remedies for neighbour disputes are only taken as a last resort when all other methods have been explored. Interviews with officers confirmed that achieving a resolution without recourse to legal action is preferable in most cases. Housing organisations and individual housing officers reported using a range of strategies to achieve a non-legal resolution to the problem including:

- the use of mediation undertaken either by an independent agency or by housing officers;

- rapid response to complaints involving use of letters, personal visits, in-depth investigations, use of compromise techniques, education and support;

- on occasions contact with tenants resulted in terminations and abandonment.

Chart 4: Median recorded complaints and NSPs served per 1,000 tenancies during 1997/98

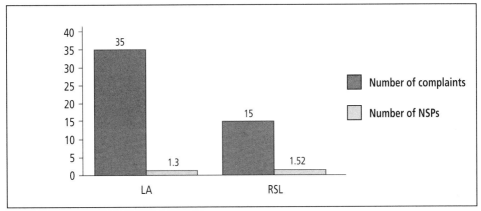

Number of respondents: *LA (1997/98)=76. RSL (1997/98)=68.* Source: *Sub-sample 2*

❏ Mediation

The study did not include a detailed investigation of mediation, but officers volunteered that mediation could be being a successful method of dealing with some anti-social behaviour complaints. Whilst mediation, either from an outside agency or from an in-house service, would often be offered or suggested by officers, it had a very variable take up and success rate. Some organisations reported that tenants were not keen to participate in mediation. However, in one organisation, mediation, for suitable one-to-one neighbour problems, was virtually mandatory or else officers would close the case. Further details about the use of mediation to resolve neighbour complaints is available in a comprehensive report on the use of mediation services (Dignan, *et al.*, 1996).

❏ Early intervention

As well as the involvement of different agencies (see Chapter 5), landlords stated that one of the key elements in reducing the need for legal action was the ability of housing officers to intervene early enough into the life cycle of the problem and 'nip things in the bud'.

> *"A lot of referrals we get are…about clash of lifestyles more than anything, and we are able to maybe get the parties to compromise and make them realise exactly what their behaviour is doing to their neighbours…It's young people, particularly, it's about educating them. It doesn't always work but it does work in some cases.*

> *So I think we're quite successful really in trying to avert the need for legal action."*

Officers reported that they would routinely respond to complaints by the use of a combination of personal visits along with warning letters. Maintaining the confidentiality of the complainant could be problematic. Whilst officers acknowledged the importance of not revealing the identity of the original complainant to the alleged perpetrator, on occasions they found it difficult to maintain this confidentiality. Complainants were also encouraged to contact their neighbours themselves, but if this was not possible most landlords said that housing officers would try and negotiate with both parties.

> *"I've found that if I go round and speak to both parties and do a bit of mediation myself...And often when the landlord gets involved...some people really take note of that..."*

One landlord reported that it was the organisation's policy for housing officers to visit people within a day of the initial complaint being made. Sometimes, however, such action was not effective in preventing legal action either because of the severity of the behaviour, or because the situation had become too entrenched by the time the landlord was notified of the problem.

Notwithstanding detailed policy procedure manuals, which emphasised the need for early intervention, the amount of preliminary and investigative work actually undertaken by housing officers was not always clear. Analysis of the information recorded on tenancy files showed that most commonly landlords simply wrote to perpetrators asking them to cease the disturbing behaviour. In two out of every five cases (40 per cent) the perpetrators were not even visited by a housing officer and in only one in five cases (19 per cent) were referrals made to other agencies. Most surprisingly, the survey showed that in less than one in five cases (18 per cent) was any reference made to the use of mediation services.

There was recognition amongst many legal and senior housing officers that front line housing officers' skills to deal with anti-social behaviour cases varied considerably, some being perfectly able, whilst others were very poor. The inconsistency of commitment, ability and training amongst housing officers were cited as causes of mismanagement and inappropriate legal action taken in some cases. In addition, pressure of other work, such as dealing with rent arrears, voids and rent collection could limit the amount of time that officers had available to deal with neighbour nuisance problems.

One senior officer referred to the culture of some of the 'old school' of housing officers, who left things to fester.

"What we're trying to do is break the culture...Some officers who are from the old school, who shied away once, found a quiet cubby hole, and just sent out letters rather than dealt with the situation."

One defence lawyer gave examples of cases where very little, if any, preliminary investigations were completed before Notices of Seeking Possession were served. Another illustrated the dangers that can occur when officers allow their prejudices to decide the course of action.

"It's the one who puts the first complaint in that has the psychological advantage straight away. The big problem with housing officers, they'll know people on the estate, people will gossip to them...I'm talking about the normal every day housing officer and [it's] based on what she thinks that starts the process off."

Inadequacies in the implementation of landlords' written policies and procedures were also highlighted by the detailed accounts given by both complainants and defendants (see Chapter 10). On occasions, complainants reported feeling very dissatisfied particularly where some preliminary action had been taken but subsequently no further intervention was forthcoming even though the anti-social behaviour continued.

On the other hand, case study landlords were also able to provide examples of very committed working practices, with officers prepared to work outside of normal hours to give households support, to try to resolve the problem and avoid the necessity of legal action. Having a locally based housing office was also cited as being helpful in identifying problems at an early stage, and made it easier for officers to keep on top of the situation.

❑ Termination and abandonment

Not infrequently front line officers reported that following intervention of some sort, usually either a letter or personal visit, problems could be 'resolved' by tenants (both those affected by the problems as well as the perpetrators) simply terminating or even abandoning their tenancies. Such action was mostly likely to occur in areas of low demand where alternative accommodation was readily available.

"There's such a lack of demand in some of our areas, if the police start calling round to people's houses, raiding tenants' properties, you quickly find that they move on somewhere else. So it's almost done your job for you. I think that's quite handy in cases, particularly where we're dealing with drug dealing, where we've got to be very careful about our own staff intervening with what could be very dangerous situation."

Indeed one landlord, located in the North of the country, reported that up to 50 per cent of cases in one neighbourhood were 'solved' in that way. Another housing officer based in the North East reported that households dealing in drugs were most likely to abandon the property before a notice was served.

❑ Summary

Generally strategies employed by landlords to avoid the necessity of taking legal action were very effective. On occasions, however, pressure of other work, and a lack of confidence, skills and expertise amongst housing officers were barriers to achieving a satisfactory resolution to the problem.

CHAPTER 8

COMMENCING LEGAL ACTION

In order to obtain possession landlords must first serve a Notice of Seeking Possession (NSP). The survey results show that both local authorities and registered social landlords used NSPs in a similar number of cases and that over the period 1996/97 to 1997/98 there had been significant increases in the median number of NSPs issued by both types of landlord. For registered social landlords there had been an increase of 126 per cent in NSPs per 1,000 tenancies whilst for local authorities the increase was found to be 113 per cent.

Chart 5: The median number of NSPs served per 1,000 tenancies (1996/97 and 1997/98)

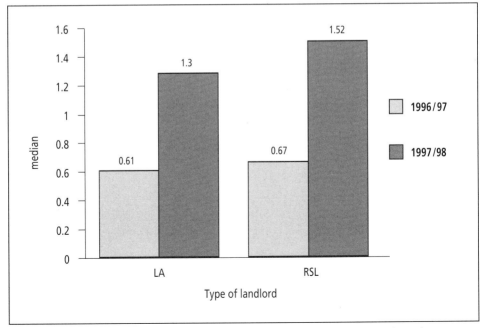

Number of respondents: *LA (1996/97)=61; (1997/98)=76. RSL (1996/97)=61; (1997/98)=68.* Source: *Sub-sample 2*

The person who made the decision to issue a NSP varied between organisations. For some it was a decision taken jointly, in-house, by the front line housing officer and their manager, only referring to their legal representative for assistance on the wording of the notice. In other organisations, the decision was made in conjunction with the legal representatives. Where solicitors were involved in deciding whether or not to issue a notice, greater emphasis was placed on the collection of sufficient evidence to pursue possession if the offending behaviour did not cease. Regardless of who made the formal decision to proceed with a NSP there was some evidence to suggest that the high profile of anti-social behaviour cases had made housing officers more nervous of acting without legal advice.

Data from the case study landlords confirmed the survey result in so far as most neighbour nuisance complaints were dealt with without recourse to NSPs. When they were employed they were found to be used in a variety of ways depending both on the nature of the problem behaviour and on the role of legal action within the overall strategy adopted by individual organisations. Generally, housing officers stated they only consider issuing NSPs in either very serious cases or where nuisance behaviour had persisted over time and other attempts to deal with the issue had failed.

In tackling anti-social behaviour, housing professionals are subject to conflicting pressures. On the one hand they are in the business of providing and managing homes for people in need, giving priority to the task of sustaining tenancies, on the other hand there is a pressure to take legal action against perpetrators of anti-social behaviour, both to protect their interests as landlords and to defend the right of other tenants to quiet enjoyment of their homes. In part, the use of NSPs were seen as a way of meeting both sets of obligations. They could be used to show other tenants that anti-social behaviour would not be tolerated: *"It's a message to the 99 per cent of the community who want to live peacefully, you know, that yes, we are doing something."* But at the same time they could also be used to provide the perpetrators with a last opportunity to change their behaviour. This dual role for NSPs is illustrated in the following comment made by a senior housing officer:

> *"The Notice of Seeking Possession…I suppose, we've failed if we've got to that stage, that's one way of looking at it. The other way of looking at it, is it's a very, very necessary tool to use perhaps early on to make it clear to the tenant that we*

*mean business and this is the way we're going to go if you don't stop doing
whatever it is you're doing."*

That eviction was a failure was reinforced by another comment:

*"The business that we're involved in is certainly not the business of evicting
tenants. I can't say that I think the eviction of a tenant is a failure, because it
certainly would come at the end of quite a long process and it certainly wouldn't
constitute a failure for the tenants who had been suffering the anti-social
behaviour. But I think it is very hard for any professional housing officer not to
see any eviction as anything that is not in some part a failure."*

The use of NSPs is illustrated by findings from the defendant case survey. In
the 56 cases where an NSP had been issued, 25 cases had subsequently been
served with a second notice and in one case five separate notices had been
served. The reasons why more than one notice may be used varied according
to the individual circumstance of the case but the fact that more than one
notice is frequently required, serves to illustrate the difficulties and
complexities evident in such cases. They do not follow a simple linear course;
behaviour erupts on different occasions, different neighbours will have
different tolerances, perpetrators may have mental health or other problems
which impact on the decision to proceed with a possession summons.

As this illustrates, the service of an NSP does not always lead to the issuing of
legal proceedings and in the following section of the report we examine the
factors that influence the decision to take further action, namely:

- the deterrent value of Notices of Seeking Possession;
- abandonment;
- the problems of evidence collection.

❑ The deterrent value of Notices of Seeking Possession

Officers reported that NSPs could be an effective way of stopping anti-social
behaviour by providing tenants with a final warning that unless the
offending behaviour ceases, eviction action will be taken. As one officer
explained:

*"Initially I would use it as a deterrent and hopefully that would be enough to stop
the problem."*

In some cases, particularly those involving vulnerable households, NSPs were seen in part to act as a deterrent simply because they demonstrated to other agencies the seriousness of the situation and prompted greater inter-agency intervention (see further Chapter 5).

Although all the landlords acknowledged that service of an NSP might be used as a deterrent and would often be sufficient to stop the problem behaviour, they also stated that it was rare for notices to be served unless sufficient evidence had been collected to proceed with court action if necessary. More frequently, in theory at least, NSPs were used with a commitment to taking further legal action if the nuisance behaviour did not cease. In some circumstances, frequently involving very serious criminal, drug related or violent behaviour, NSPs were used with the explicit intention of issuing possession proceedings. One officer summarised the different use of NSPs in the following way:

> "So there are those situations where it's to draw the line in the sand and make clear that anything further is going to lead to legal action, and other situations where serving the notice is in fact saying to that person, 'right, legal action is now going to be taken and this is the first step in the process'."

Officers were also aware that more stringent use was made of NSPs in anti-social behaviour cases, as compared to practices in relation to rent arrears cases. They explained how in rent arrears cases the notice was often served without a clear intention of taking subsequent action but in anti-social behaviour cases there was usually a commitment to take further action if the behaviour complained about did not cease:

> "In anti-social behaviour cases…it's not…like rents where we serve quite a lot of notices on rents simply to get them to pay [and] really no intention of taking them to court. I think with notices on anti-social behaviour you've got to be a little bit more careful that you're not serving them like confetti."

Despite housing officers' views, some lawyers acknowledged that in practice it was not uncommon for notices to be used primarily as deterrents. One private solicitor, with experience of many registered social landlords, said he had many cases where an NSP had been served before he got the case and where there had been little intent to follow through and little understanding of the proper procedure.

❏ Abandonment

A further important reason why NSPs did not always result in subsequent legal action was the fact that on a number of occasions, as with letters and visits, they led to voluntary abandonment of the tenancy. As one officer explained:

> *"The person leaves because they know that they are causing such a problem that they're going to lose out anyway, so they don't want to go to court, so they just go."*

Abandonment appeared to be a particular feature in the case studies based in the North East and North West, although there was also evidence of it occurring to a lesser extent in London. While this result could be seen as effective, in so far as it may stop nuisance behaviour in a particular locality, some officers expressed concern that in practice it was likely to simply represent a displacement of the problem to another area or landlord rather than a long-term resolution of the problem (see Chapter 13).

❏ Problems of evidence collection

The final set of reasons given for cases not proceeding to possession action following the service of a NSP, concerned the difficulties many landlords reported in collecting sufficient evidence to support a summons. Access to detailed evidence is crucial to the success of a case in court, yet housing officers felt plagued by a range of obstacles at all stages in the evidence collection process. The case study data provides many reasons and examples of the type of difficulties encountered. They include:

- reluctance of tenants to be witnesses;
- fear of intimidation;
- difficulties of collecting the appropriate quality of evidence;
- fear of the court;
- length of time;
- lack of training for housing officers.

Reluctance of tenants to get involved as witnesses in legal proceedings
Producing evidence of the standard required for court requires housing officers to develop specialist skills. The most obvious source of such evidence

is complainants who must be prepared and able to keep incident diaries, give detailed statements, attend court hearings and provide formal evidence. Without exception, officers reported difficulties in finding neighbours and other witnesses prepared to come forward at the NSP stage of the possession process, let alone stay the course to a final trial. Similar problems in collecting evidence and persuading people to act as witnesses were noted in an earlier study on racial harassment (Dhooge and Barelli, 1996). One officer's description spoke for many:

> *"[It's] the biggest problem we've got…I mean you've got the evidence, you know everything…but then they say: 'But I won't attend court'."*

Officers' perceptions as to why neighbours and complainants were reluctant to get involved in formal action varied, but most commonly included the following factors:

- many potential witnesses are themselves vulnerable and find it difficult to be articulate in formal and unfamiliar situations;
- the legal process is intimidating to tenants who fear the court process and the requirement to give evidence in person;
- people get fed up by the process of regular diary keeping and lose confidence that anything will be done;
- the length of time it can take to get cases to trial can also acts as a deterrent for many witnesses;
- general tenant apathy.

In addition to the above factors, the survey findings indicated that witness intimidation was a key issue for social landlords with just under six out of ten landlords stating that on at least one occasion witnesses in anti-social behaviour cases had been subject to intimidation. Interestingly, interviews with both housing officers and solicitors showed that while in a some cases witnesses had been subject to abuse and serious intimidation, it was also the *fear* of intimidation which played a powerful role in discouraging potential witnesses from getting involved, as one officer explained:

> *"There is some intimidation that does go on but I think in the main it's the fear of the intimidation not the actual intimidation."*

Tenants interviewed had a very different view of witness intimidation (see Chapter 10). Most of the intimidation these tenants experienced was real enough, resulting in verbal abuse, damage to property, physical retaliation and occasionally violent attacks. On the whole tenants felt let down by their landlord as little had been done to prevent such retaliation and intimidation. The best evidence of support came from tenants of landlords who had access to specialist units or officers. Nevertheless, even where a landlord has exhibited exemplary practice, including supportive police action, there is a limit to the amount of supportive action that can be undertaken in cases where there is severe harassment from the start of evidence collection through to the final trial.

Practical support measures

A wide variety of methods and strategies, to counteract the particular difficulties encountered in persuading neighbours to become involved as witnesses were identified.

It was felt that the most effective action that housing organisations could take was to provide a range of support measures operating at a collective and community level as well as at an individual level. Good practice in evidence collection methods, identified by the case study organisations, included both practical measures to support tenants and improve the quality of evidence collected and psychological support to promote confidence amongst individuals and the community as a whole.

Witness support measures

- Large scale door knocking to make contact with all those potentially affected by the anti-social behaviour and arranging to meet groups of neighbours can result in more evidence and provides individuals with group support.
- Use of 'neighbourhood letters' to encourage other witnesses to come forward.
- Maintaining close contact with neighbours and witnesses by use of regular visits in order to build up trust and support.
- Being realistic about the process and the possible outcome, whilst recognising their fears – allowing witnesses to weigh up the situation realistically.
- Measures to ensure that wherever possible individual complainant details are not revealed to the perpetrators. Complainant confidentiality was found to be very important in building tenants' confidence to act as witnesses.

→

- Use of injunctions to ensure that witnesses feel protected from intimidation.
- Arranging for the organisation's solicitor or legal officer to visit individual witnesses or groups of witnesses, in their homes, to explain the court process and provide continuing support.
- Arranging for witnesses to be taken on accompanied visits to the court prior to the hearing.
- Offering witnesses temporary alternative accommodation during the lead up to the trial. Some landlords also offer alternative permanent accommodation to witnesses, but this can result in potential witnesses withdrawing their evidence once rehoused.
- Provision of mobile phones, alarms and extra physical security measures.

Where the methods outlined above had been employed, housing officers reported that witnesses were more likely to come forward. One solicitor commented that it was necessary to start out with four or five potential witnesses in the hopes that one or two good witnesses would be prepared to testify at the final court hearing. One organisation reported that they had never had a problem securing the co-operation of witnesses because they offered, *"absolute support"*:

> *"The first thing is education, information. Explaining to them in simple terms precisely what will happen and leading them through it, keeping in contact. Where there is a risk…we always carry out a risk assessment with the police… that there may be some intimidation we offer them…victim support, the police putting in some form of equipment or if the situation merited it having an injunction put in place whilst the possession proceedings are ongoing, purely as a witness support measure."*

Specialist units come into their own in this kind of work, as they have the staff, resources and commitment to ensure maximum support and encouragement. There was much respect and praise for the bravery of many of the witnesses who persevere in giving evidence despite some fearful conditions.

Lack of training and support for housing officers

Some of the case study organisations found the process of evidence collection more problematic than others. This suggests that the difficulties may be exacerbated by housing officers' lack of skill, training and knowledge, in conjunction with the lack of support and direction within the organisation's culture. Solicitors still had to convince housing officers of the importance of proper evidence collection and that reliance on hearsay was not enough.

Even where an organisation has a specialist unit there can still be problems in ensuring front line officers have the required skills. As one officer commented:

"I think housing officers at the moment have got a very difficult job because this kind of work has evolved really and a lot of the staff who are on the front line now who have been in the job a long time didn't used to do this sort of work. Suddenly here they are in the middle of it, not necessarily…being equipped with all the necessary skills."

It was clear that there was great inconsistency amongst officers in their experience and knowledge about the standard required for the compilation of witness statements and other admissible evidence. While individual officers within an organisation may be very committed to developing the required skills, and exhibited good practice, in general, organisations' legal advisors felt that officers had relatively little experience in collecting evidence and had received little ongoing training. This was exemplified in interviews with tenant complainants (see Chapter 10).

For the lawyers, it was the strength of the evidence that made a case or not, and they had to be at least 100 per cent confident of it, something which it was felt housing officers did not quite fully appreciate. For instance, one private solicitor commented:

"The housing officers, or the managers, really don't know what to do. They might have an inkling of where they should be going, but they just really want you to sort it out."

Despite these criticisms, lawyers interviewed perceived there to be improvements in housing officers' understanding of the range of preliminary work that was necessary in order to take legal action. They felt officers had gained more confidence and knowledge since the 1996 Housing Act had been introduced and were better placed to start building a case.

A few of the case study organisations provided front line officers with clear procedures, accessible legal support, and ongoing training. Where such positive support was available, either through a specialist unit, or specialist officer, front line officers stated that their confidence to tackle difficult cases had increased. There was also some evidence that provision of training and back up support for officers helped to build confidence amongst potential witnesses that the organisation had the ability to take effective action. However, not all organisations felt they were in a position to provide officers with specialist support, either because the scale of the problem was too small to justify such resource intensive action, or because the structure of the organisation, devolved over many regions and areas, made it difficult. This was a particular problem for some of the registered social landlords and for the smaller organisations.

Alternative methods of evidence collection

The survey found that in response to the difficulties experienced in collecting evidence directly from neighbours, the use of professional or third party witnesses, such as housing and environmental health officers, the police and in some cases private investigators was common. Over half of registered social landlords (54 per cent) and nearly three-quarters (73 per cent) of local authorities stated that they had used professionals to give evidence in court.

The case study organisations' views on the value of professional witnesses were mixed. The problems of obtaining evidence from the police have already been discussed in Chapter 5, although where it could be obtained it was seen as the best possible evidence. Less enthusiasm was expressed about the use of professional investigators as witnesses in court. Common criticisms focussed on the expense involved and the difficulty of employing professionals to monitor anti-social behaviour which was not predictable leading to very 'hit and miss' results. As one officer stated: *"Professional witnesses, in practical terms there might be one in a million cases where they would be feasible."* Doubts were also expressed by a private solicitor over the value of having professional witnesses in court and he thought that generally judges were not impressed with their evidence. Only one organisation regularly used professional witnesses to give evidence in court. More commonly professional witnesses and third party witnesses were used by organisations to establish the scale of the problem and to collect evidence to challenge perpetrators in a last attempt to get them to change their behaviour.

Other alternative methods of evidence collection were also identified. Where landlords had access to specialist officers or the services of TEST, an out of hours service was often provided, which could be invaluable in terms of evidence collection (see Chapter 6). Alternatively the use of camcorders and CCTV were proving valuable, not necessarily to be used in court, but to confirm that a particular problem existed and to establish who the perpetrators were. In one of the case study organisations, a tenants' and residents' association felt so strongly about the need to tackle anti-social behaviour that they held jumble sales and other fund raising events in order to purchase a camcorder for the local housing office. The local housing officer then explained how the camcorder had been used as a way of confronting a perpetrator: *"We actually went and showed them what we had filmed on the camcorder and we said: 'we need to take you to court. Do you want us to take you to court or do you want to sign this termination form?'"* One solicitor remarked how he had taken one case on video evidence alone.

> *"If one has good quality video evidence, it's very hard to argue against. It can often take the place of a witness having to give evidence of their own experience, having to go through that ordeal of giving evidence and hoping it will be believed. If there's a video tape there that proves the basic complaint, be it noise or violence etc…I think it is also quite a powerful tool in court – the use of sound and pictures is quite compelling."*

Another in-house solicitor praised the use of photographs which were often taken by a housing officer using a digital camera. These have never been disputed in court.

❏ Summary

NSPs were used for a variety of different purposes with relatively few cases leading to subsequent possession action. In some cases NSPs were reported as being effective in stopping nuisance behaviour or had resulted in the perpetrator abandoning the tenancy, but in other cases difficulties in obtaining evidence prevented any further legal action being taken.

CHAPTER 9

LEGAL REMEDIES AT COURT

The following section of the report focusses on the use of legal remedies at court, i.e. possession orders and injunctions. The case study organisations were asked about their views on:

- the value of possession proceedings and the type of outcomes sought from the courts;

- the extent, to which injunctions were used, either in conjunction with possession actions or as a stand-alone measure;

- difficulties encountered in the court process.

Generally, amongst the case study landlords, the decision to take legal action was made jointly by the housing officer, their manager and a lawyer, with most weight given to the housing officer's views. One landlord involved a police liaison officer in regular project team meetings, which monitored cases. For local authority landlords, politicians were also sometimes involved in the decision as to whether to take legal action. Although lawyers were rarely responsible for the final decision, their advice was influential in determining the outcome. One private lawyer found that many of his clients often called when things were, *"out of control"* with people *"screaming for a resolution."* All landlords reported there were sometimes differences of opinion over the route to be taken, which led to tensions, particularly when political interference by councillors was seen as pressuring officers and lawyers to take what they felt might be inappropriate measures. To lose a case was seen as being, *"twice as bad"* as not taking the case in the first instance.

❑ Use of possession proceedings

The survey showed that over the two-year period 1996-98 there had been a 127 per cent increase in possession actions taken on anti-social behaviour

Chart 6: Increase in court actions for possession per 1,000 tenancies between 1996/97 and 1997/98 – local authorities

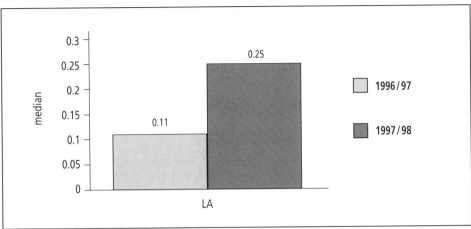

Number of respondents: *LAs (1996/97)=67; (1997/98)=87.* Source: Sub-sample 2

grounds by local authorities. It was more difficult to measure registered social landlords' use of possession action because of deficiencies in their monitoring systems.

The case study data confirmed that both types of landlord were prepared to take eviction action to deal with anti-social behaviour, but as with the serving of NSPs, views on the merits of taking possession action varied. Some landlords felt it was the most effective way of dealing with anti-social behaviour; as one officer commented:

"Obviously possession orders eradicate the problem locally and it sends really good signals to the people on the estate. They can see that the landlords' actually doing something."

For others, this form of action was only used as a last resort, the 'ultimate sanction', when all other attempts to resolve the problem had failed or where confidence in the wider neighbourhood needed to be restored:

"Possession is basically the last resort because at the end of the day all you're doing is moving the problem elsewhere…Possession in itself, obviously, has all sorts of spin offs which might benefit the community in terms of sending a message out to people that this won't be tolerated, that the housing department will take action against perpetrators of nuisance…But I think injunctions and working with other agencies is one of the best ways perhaps of trying to avoid possession".

There was some evidence that on occasions, in order to ensure that the possession action was successful and some sort of possession order, albeit a suspended one, was achieved, landlords would take a strategic decision to take action on the grounds of rent arrears as well as or instead of the rather more complex grounds of neighbour nuisance. The following excerpts from a case note written by a solicitor to a housing officer demonstrates the complex process required to weigh up the advantages and disadvantages of using the different grounds for possession:

> *"I reiterated to him my view that the current evidence was not...sufficient for us to be confident of getting an order against [Ms X] on nuisance grounds. I advised him this was a difficult judgement to make but having regard to the fact that the local authority would treat her as intentionally homeless I did not feel the evidence was sufficiently compelling for me to be confident of a result. We talked about tactics and for PR reasons, it is very important that if [Ms X] goes we need her to go under the cloud of nuisance. It was agreed therefore that I would prepare a NSP using ground 12 and 14 as well as ground 8 [rent arrears]. It was also agreed that possession proceedings would be issued on all allegations recognising that in relation to the nuisance part of the case we may well have to pull the action if by some means [Ms X] gets enough money together to defeat the ground 8 claim."*

Outcomes

When a possession case comes to court, four outcomes are possible: dismissal, adjournment, suspended possession or outright possession. Both the survey results and the case study landlords clearly show that where the decision was taken to take possession action on the grounds of anti-social behaviour landlords were most likely to obtain an outright order. Charts 7 and 8 show that over the period 1997/98, an outright order for possession was granted in 58 per cent of local authority cases and 52 per cent of registered social landlord cases. A similar pattern of outcomes was found in the defendant case study survey, where, of the 30 cases that proceeded to final hearing, 53 per cent resulted in an outright order for possession.

What is less clear from these findings is whether, in taking possession action, landlords' prime objective was to evict the perpetrators. In the case study interviews, we were interested to establish what type of orders were sought from the courts, whether landlords always sought outright orders, or whether there were circumstances in which a suspended order would be requested. The evidence from the case study organisations on this issue was somewhat mixed.

Chart 7: Outcomes of possession proceedings – local authorities

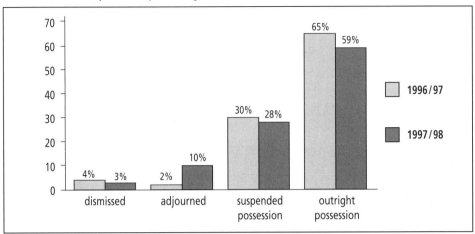

Number of respondents: Sub-sample 1. *LAs (1996/97)=31; (1997/98)=58* Number of possession cases: *1996/97=113; 1997/98=250*

Chart 8: Outcomes of possession proceedings – RSLs

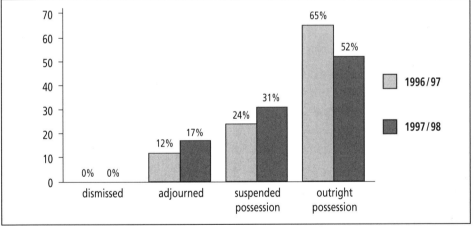

Number of respondents: Sub-sample 1. *RSLs (1996/97)=20; (1997/98)=33* Number of possession cases: *1996/97=34; 1997/98=52*

For some landlords once a decision was taken to proceed with possession action, there was a tendency to adopt a hard line approach and actively seek to evict the perpetrators. As one officer explained:

> *"If it's got as far as the court on a nuisance case, then…our expectation would be for an outright order, for immediate possession, because it must have been so bad for it to have got to court."*

It was clear that in cases involving extremely disturbing anti-social behaviour, the granting of an outright order could resolve major management problems on an estate and ensure more efficient use of resources, as the following comment illustrates:

> "I have had no problems on that estate since we got the eviction. It's like a normal estate, it's wonderful. But that estate took up so much of my officers' time, my time and it's like the resources that have been released in evicting one family, it's just incredible, really incredible."

In other cases, however, it was questionable as to whether such a hard line approach was appropriate. For example, in one case the anti-social behaviour had been committed almost exclusively by the tenants' partner. Not only was he abusive to the neighbours, but he was also abusive and violent towards the tenant, and had caused damage to the property. He was in due course arrested for criminal offences and it was predicted that he would receive a custodial sentence, thus ending the majority of the problems. The landlord nonetheless pressed for an outright possession order. The reason for this was noted on the tenancy file:

> "[The tenant] had shown no remorse for the damage [her partner] had caused nor indeed had she taken any steps to prevent it."

Misgivings expressed about the use of suspended orders focussed on the negative effect such orders had on neighbouring tenants, who might believe that they had been let down by the landlord and the difficulty experienced in persuading witnesses to return to court to testify if the terms of the suspended order were breached:

> "I think...suspended possession order[s] on anti-social behaviour are a disaster...I think you've lost your witnesses. You've got your witness suffering still from harassment or nuisance or whatever, and now he's being told: 'well we're giving him [the perpetrator] one more chance' and that witness probably knows he's never going to change and he'll give up."

This view was echoed by one unhappy tenant and her family, who had been forced to completely change their lives by moving to another part of town. Following the traumas of the court process and long waits for action, they subsequently felt that it all had been a waste of time since the perpetrator was still in her home, with no other apparent sanction imposed to stop the anti-social behaviour. In fact, most suspended orders do provide sanctions in so far as such orders are usually made subject to specific conditions. For example, in one case the major complaints concerned using the property as a garage business, which led to noise and disturbance to neighbours. The garage had been erected by the tenant without the necessary planning consents and was in fact in a dangerous condition. The landlord obtained a very detailed suspended order, which was complied with, in the following terms:

> *"To dismantle garage within 28 days*
> *No other structures to be erected without permission*
> *No vehicles/part of to be stored/parked on the curtilage after 28 days*
> *No repairs/maintenance within the curtilage or immediate locality*
> *No nuisance/annoyance to neighbours*
> *No harassment/intimidation of neighbours*
> *Allowed to park one vehicle of own registration to be given to the housing office*
> *Allowed to repair that vehicle 10 a.m. – 4 p.m. as long as not a nuisance."*

In order to avoid a sense that suspended orders are a failure the detailed conditions need to be carefully explained to both the complainants and the perpetrators.

Notwithstanding both landlords' and tenants' reservations about suspended orders and the apparent advantages of outright orders, a number of landlords took a more pragmatic approach to the outcome sought from the courts stating that each case was dealt with individually.

> *"So each case is looked at on its individual merits…at times we are satisfied with a suspended order, at times we look for absolute, because we feel that the only solution to this problem is to remove that family from our estate."*

Two organisations indicated that they saw a positive role for suspended orders and in the future would be making greater use of them in conjunction with an increasing use of injunctions. For these landlords the most important consideration was the desire to stop the offending behaviour:

> *"Ultimately I'm looking to prevent the problem and to protect the safety of… residents in the area and if that can be achieved by undertaking a suspended order then that's a good result. If the only way for that to be achieved is an immediate possession order then that's a successful result."*

One solicitor commented that suspended orders would occasionally be sought as a tactical bargaining move to save them from having to undertake an expensive and long defended trial. Other reasons given as to why, on occasions, a suspended order would be an acceptable outcome focussed on where the perpetrators had left the property, perhaps as a result of a custodial sentence, where the offending behaviour had stopped, or in cases where there was insufficient evidence to secure an outright order. One officer described a situation where: *"the problems are horrendous but we can't get enough evidence and we certainly can't get enough recent evidence and so the best course of action is a suspended order."*

❏ Defence solicitors' views on possession proceedings

Defence lawyers stated that in their experience landlords frequently took a hard line approach in anti-social behaviour cases. Defending such cases usually focussed on ensuring that defendants did not lose their homes. Although initially a dismissal would be sought, most of the defence lawyers said they would be happy to accept a suspended possession order. Defence lawyers stated they usually tried to negotiate an arrangement before trial but they reported that this was often difficult to achieve because of the 'unreasonableness' of officers, particularly legal officers. Housing officers were more amenable to negotiation, but once the case was in the hands of the legal officers then a more 'bullish' approach tended to be taken.

The main focus for the defence was challenging the 'reasonableness' of the action[1]:

> *"Reasonableness is usually the most fertile ground for a housing lawyer, in as much as that I'd want to know her personal circumstance, children, local schools, whether they go to a local church, local community centre, whether they've got ill health etc. etc."*

Many examples were given where landlords had been defeated in court, or had to drop cases, because they could not demonstrate to the court that it was reasonable to grant possession. Defence lawyers often sought to establish lack of reasonableness by getting evidence of neighbours' support for the defendants, for example by knocking on doors in the neighbourhood, getting petitions signed and arranging witnesses for the defence.

The strongest objections by defence lawyers to legal action being taken against their clients were reserved for the cases where clients had been

---

1. Possession can only be granted under the relevant grounds if the court considers it 'reasonable' to do so.

threatened with eviction as a result of a criminal conviction. In such cases, defendants were seen as being punished twice. Not only had they served a prison sentence but they were also threatened with the loss of their home. Although criminal convictions may constitute a ground for possession, it was felt most strongly that consideration of this action should happen at the criminal trial in front of a judge, so the two elements could be heard together. The experiences of tenants convicted of offences are illustrated in Chapter 10.

❑ Use of injunctions

In theory, injunctions have several advantages over possession proceedings in that they can be more quickly obtained on an interim basis and are addressed to specific individuals to cease specific behaviours. They also have the advantage of enabling landlords to take action against anti-social behaviour without eviction proceedings being used. In practice, however, the survey and cases study findings confirmed earlier anecdotal evidence which suggested that, while a few landlords frequently used injunctions as a method of dealing with neighbour nuisance, many others rarely use this remedy. Despite the apparent advantages of injunctions and the Housing Act 1996 provisions strengthening the use of this remedy, in fact very few of the survey landlords could provide any detailed information about cases in which this remedy had been employed. Indeed, the very small number of injunctions requested by registered social landlords prevents a detailed analysis of trends for these landlords.

Frequently landlords' stated policy on the use of injunctions appeared to be at variance with the actual use of injunctions. Detailed examination of action taken in individual cases showed that even where landlords said they would use injunctions, in practice it was a remedy that was rarely employed. Overall, just under two-thirds of local authorities stated they were prepared to use injunctions sometimes or always, with nine out of ten (93 per cent) metropolitan authorities stating they would use this remedy. Most registered social landlords on the other hand rarely or never used injunctions. It appeared that registered social landlords with a stock size of less than 1,499 were least likely to use this remedy with over half (52 per cent) stating they *never* used injunctions as compared to four out of five (82 per cent) of the largest landlords (those with stock size of 10,000 plus) who stated they sometimes used this remedy.

In 1997/98, of the 30 local authority housing departments who reported using injunctions for breach of tenancy, half (16) had also made use of the provisions for obtaining injunctions under the Housing Act 1996. It appears that the new measures introduced under the 1996 Housing Act, which came into effect in September 1997 are predominantly being used by those who are familiar with the legal process associated with injunctions and are not in practice being used by the majority of social landlords.

The interviews with the case study landlords and their legal representatives, probed their perception of the value of injunctions, in what circumstances they were used, and if they were not used at all, why.

Conflicting views

The results showed that there were widely conflicting views held about injunctions. With the exception of one landlord, most of the case study organisations had relatively little or no experience of using injunctions. Where they did use them, it was invariably in conjunction with possession proceedings. In the one organisation which used injunctions as the main form of legal action in four out of five cases, both the front line and senior officers felt them to be a more effective and valuable method of resolving the problem of anti-social behaviour than possession action. As one of the officers put it:

> "Well, I think injunctions are the real business of tackling anti-social behaviour. If your aim is to…end the behaviour then the injunction provides you with an urgent immediate relief for your organisation. So, I think it's a very full and quick response to anti-social behaviour. And the other thing is it is effective. We don't subsequently have to go to the process of seeking possession."

In contrast to this very positive view of injunctive action, many registered social landlords in the case study sample expressed doubts about their value. The following comment is fairly typical of such landlords:

> "I would say injunctions are ineffective in our cases. It just settles the situation down for a number of months, but the same behaviour will come through eventually."

Another officer expressed a preference for possession proceedings stating that:

> "We find the route of taking a Notice of Seeking Possession and taking people either to get an undertaking in terms of a suspended possession order is as powerful as going for an injunction. We haven't to date any cases where we felt [an injunction] was merited."

These views were reflected in interviews with private solicitors, who felt that their clients preferred route was possession.

Solicitors were more likely to use injunctions where violence was an issue, but still as part of a possession action. There had been very little use of injunctions against non-tenants. The low uptake of injunctions was in part attributed to the perceived difficulties in their enforcement. Some lawyers had experience of applying for powers of arrest to be attached to the original order and this was found to greatly improve their effectiveness, but committal proceedings were seen by both housing officers and legal representatives to be expensive and problematic, with the need to have the understanding and co-operation of the police and willing witnesses. It was felt that judges would not always take the matter seriously:

> "Is a judge going to jail somebody for contempt of court for repairing their car? Chances are, probably not!"

One tenant found herself having to explain to the local police force and get papers to convince them that her neighbour had had an injunction served, which was now breached. Seen from the other side, however, the defendant could be seen to be in a disadvantageous position when trying to obtain legal representation at such short notice when issued with a committal summons with power of arrest.

Contradictory understanding of the role of injunctions

Further analysis of the case study interview data showed there to be widely contradictory perceptions as to how injunctions could be used. For example, in an organisation that did not use injunctions it was stated that they would not be an appropriate method of dealing with noise nuisance,

> "I think a lot of the time the nuisance problems that we've been having haven't been the sort where you could use an injunction. I think they're much more applicable to ones where you've got threatening behaviour involving people who are intimidating. I don't think that excessive amounts of noise and nuisance are ones where that's really appropriate. I mean, a lot of times it's where it's a clash of lifestyle. And again, I don't think that use of injunction is appropriate."

In contrast to this view, another landlord regularly used injunctions to deal with identical problems arising from life style clashes such as loud music or late night parties:

> "I think it's useful as well for people to be taken to court to actually explain to a judge why they behaved in a certain way or why the judge shouldn't grant an

injunction if they're playing loud music. Often it takes a judge, or for it to get to that stage, before people will really appreciate that there's a problem and I think that injunctions are probably the best method really that we've got at the moment."

A range of further reasons were given by landlords for not making greater use of injunctions:

- Many officers and in some cases even their legal advisors, had received little training in the use of injunctions. One officer even stated that she had not heard of any housing provider using injunctions.

- There was also a perception that injunctive action would be very expensive with no guarantee of a successful outcome. While officers commonly stated that, *"Injunctions are extremely expensive"*, in fact information on the costs of different forms of legal action suggest that injunctions are a cheaper method of taking action against perpetrators than possession action.

- Landlords were concerned about potential problems that may occur if injunctions were breached. Those who did use injunctions acknowledged that breaches can cause difficulties and that in order to resolve problems there is a need for very close working relationships with other agencies, particularly the police.

- Further concerns, expressed mostly by front line officers, focussed on the difficulties of evidence collection. In particular, it was felt that it would be very problematic to persuade neighbours to act as witnesses in injunction proceedings, when the perpetrators remained in the same locality. Yet while there were strong views that evidence for injunctions should be as robust as that for possession action, there were solicitors working for both types of landlord, who thought this was not necessary as a case did not have to be proved in quite the same way. One stated that it was not necessary to prove reasonableness, while another said: *"much quicker, just normally an affidavit of our officer. So we're not worried about any residents."*

The perception that injunctions were a less effective method of dealing with anti-social behaviour, as compared to eviction action, was not confined to officers. In two organisations there was some evidence of officers and legal representatives being put under political pressure to take eviction action rather than use injunctions, as the following comment about a high profile case illustrates:

"Looking back at it, it would not have been politically acceptable…we were told by our [political] masters basically, 'You go for eviction'…Even when legal [advisors] said 'your bottom line is you're unlikely to get an eviction you will more probably get a suspended order', we said 'what about an injunction?' [They] said: 'No you're going for an eviction'."

Although currently few landlords use injunctions, there were signs that officers were beginning to change their views on their value. The one case study landlord who used injunctions as the dominant form of legal action saw them as having an immediate effect, playing a valuable role in controlling anti-social behaviour, and strengthening the possession case if they had to go down that route. It was, however, acknowledged that good lines of communication between housing and legal officers were needed to help produce successful injunctions. A defence solicitor operating in this area was concerned, however, that sometimes cases were brought where there was, *"very little by way of complaint."*

Frequently, organisations that did not use injunctions recognised that they may be a useful remedy, but lacked the necessary knowledge or information on how they could be used. One landlord acknowledged that, *"we have not a lot of experience in injunctions – we haven't made use of them."* In organisations who used injunctions occasionally or who were considering making greater use of them in the future, they were seen as being particularly suitable in cases where perpetrators are vulnerable, e.g. where there are mental health problems.

If social landlords are to be encouraged to make greater use of injunctions as a method of dealing with a range of anti-social behaviour, there is a need for improved information dissemination about the benefits of such an approach and the provision of appropriate training for officers.

❏ Problems with courts

The survey found that in general terms landlords were positive about their working relationships with the courts, but they also expressed a number of negative views focussing on their perception of the difficulties encountered in taking anti-social behaviour cases through the court process. These same concerns were reflected in the comments made by the case study organisations.

Undue delay in the legal process

Lack of priority given to cases by the courts, resulting in prolonged delays, was perhaps the most commonly cited frustration expressed by solicitors, housing officers, and tenants alike.

The case study organisations identified two main sources of delays in the court process. The first point of delay occurred in the period between the summons being issued and a first hearing date, while the second period of delay occurred between the first hearing date and the listing of cases for full trial. Often landlords reported having to wait between two to three months for a first hearing date with further delays of between three and six months to get cases listed for full trial. It was not uncommon for organisations to report that the process could take as long as nine months from the point of issuing a summons to final trial.

Housing officers frequently expressed despair over the length of time it took to get cases in court. Only one organisation had successfully negotiated with the local court to shorten the length of time to get cases listed for full trial to approximately 12 weeks, but even in this organisation officers were frustrated by delays. Many respondents felt that the courts should give priority to anti-social behaviour cases over and above other less urgent cases, such as rent arrears cases. As one officer commented:

> *"It would be really useful if cases [based] on the grounds of anti-social behaviour are prioritised rather than go into the system…with rent arrears and others. I think they should be looked at separately by the court, and given an earlier date."*

Further evidence of the length of time it took to take cases through the court process was provided by the analysis of individual case files. The average number of weeks from summons to first hearing was eight weeks, with a range from one to 19 weeks. In a quarter of cases, it had taken over ten weeks. The average number of weeks from the first hearing to full trial was just under four months (15.5 weeks). Here again there was a wide range from one to 44 weeks. More than a third of cases took over 21 weeks from initial hearing to final trial.

Despite the evidence that long delays could be experienced, there were also examples of how quickly action could be taken where landlords wished to achieve a speedy hearing. Anne's case provides a vivid illustration of what can be achieved.

Anne

May 19, 1997: Anne moved into her tenancy. Complaints began immediately.

May 22, 1997: letter to tenant regarding complaints, and suggesting she returned keys.

May 27, 1997: letter to tenant, stating that an expedited court hearing for immediate possession was to be sought.

May 28, 1997: Notice of Seeking Possession served by leaving it at the premises.

May 28, 1997: summons for possession issued.

May 28, 1997: without notice, application before district judge to dispense with service of notice, to abridge time for service of summons, to expedite hearing, and for an injunction requiring compliance with the tenancy agreement. Application granted, with trial to be heard on June 4.

June 4, 1997: Anne sought an adjournment to obtain legal advice. Application refused, outright possession order granted, to take effect on June 5.

In this particular case the orders were overturned on appeal to the circuit judge, but it serves to illustrate how much can be achieved in speeding up a case where the landlord and their solicitors set out to do so, rather than letting the matter drift at the pace set by the courts in the normal course of events.

In addition to frustration caused by court delays, officers also cited a number of additional problems that arose as a consequence of these delays. In particular, officers reported greater difficulties in maintaining witnesses' confidence the longer the case dragged on. One landlord reported some success in counteracting the impact of delays by adopting a strategy of providing witnesses with detailed information on the likely length of time that a case would take at the start of the process. In many cases, however, officers felt that undue delay prejudiced the case, with potential witnesses either dropping out or even moving away from the area. The longer the delay to the court dates, the older and less powerful the evidence would be. It was also reported that the longer a case took to resolve, the greater the likelihood of witness intimidation.

Delays experienced due to the courts were also cited by solicitors as having caused, on occasions, cases to be dropped or adjourned, particularly where there were no further examples of anti-social behaviour. This could cause great frustration amongst tenants.

Officers acknowledged that there could be other causes of delay, but it was particularly the court system, and the apparent lack of knowledge amongst court staff of the serious and urgent nature of the cases, combined with the lack of awareness of the impact of delays on witnesses, that concerned practitioners.

Nevertheless, a few solicitors interviewed thought that their strategy of having all the evidence ready before issuing a summons helped in reducing any delay. Persistence, knowledge of the court system, and good communication with court staff were also cited by one solicitor as important in achieving an earlier listing.

For the defence, delays were more likely to be seen in a positive light, although one solicitor was vehemently against this idea. A delay allowed defendants to take stock of the situation, as well, one para-legal put it, giving them a chance to be, *"Mother Theresa"*, adding that he might instruct defendants to, *"have the best children in the world,"* in that intervening period. One defence para-legal thought that much of these delays were self-inflicted by the plaintiff, in not trying harder to find other methods, including negotiation, to resolve the problem.

Intimidatory nature of the courts

Other problems identified with the court process, focussed on the intimidatory nature of the courtroom and the judicial processes. Officers reported that witnesses frequently found giving formal evidence in court and being cross-examined, a very upsetting experience. One officer described how destructive the court process could be for witnesses:

> *"There are a few cases where we've just seen the hard won confidence of witnesses destroyed. I've seen witnesses walking out of the court more at risk than they were when they walked in because individual judges are disconnected from reality…Witnesses have left the court and said: 'I will never set foot in a court again'."*

These experiences were confirmed by the complainants interviewed (see Chapter 10).

Respondents identified a range of improvements that could be made to the court system to ensure a victim-centred approach was adopted. Some of the proposals were relatively simple, involving measures to provide witnesses with greater support and protection in court. The provision of separate seating areas for witnesses and alleged perpetrators was seen to be a priority:

> *"when we've been to court, specifically at county court, there's no witness protection scheme, like witnesses and perpetrators are expected to sit in the same waiting room, there's no protection."*

Others felt that the situation would be less frightening if cases were held in chambers. Where this had been done, the tenant's experience was much less fearful.

A more radical solution put forward by a number of landlords concerned the development of separate housing courts with specialist judges. This was seen to have the advantage of improving the level of knowledge and skill of the judiciary to deal with complex cases whilst also providing witnesses with a less intimidating environment and improving the court administration to minimise delays.

The approach of different judges

In determining the most appropriate order to make in possession hearings, judges exercise substantial judicial discretion, since the court must be satisfied that it is reasonable, taking into account all the circumstances, to grant possession. Many of the landlords' criticisms concerned judges' application of the test of 'reasonableness' as applied in anti-social behaviour cases. Some landlords and their solicitors expressed the view that in serious cases involving violence or criminal or drug related behaviour the onus of proof on the question of 'reasonableness' should be reversed, although this has effectively been achieved through some recent decisions of the Court of Appeal (see Manning, 1999).

Judges themselves also came in for criticism occasionally for their cavalier treatment of witnesses but more commonly as a result of perceived inconsistencies in approach and findings, and lack of knowledge of the relevant legislation. One private solicitor was particularly concerned about judges' lack of familiarity with the relevant law:

> *"Some judges are conversant with the workings of the Housing Act and able to reel off case law, and others haven't looked at anything remotely like a housing case…and that's very common unfortunately. This not only effects the conduct of the case and the eventual potential outcome but it also effects the speed of the trial if your judge doesn't understand the scope of that."*

Some officers perceived there to be differences in approach between district judges, who mainly dealt in family law, and circuit judges, who had more experience of criminal cases. This view was echoed by defence lawyers, one of whom commented that the district judges were perhaps less experienced and more 'nervous' and therefore would be more likely to favour the plaintiff:

> *"I've come across district judges who are nervous. You can imagine the district judges sat there in 'anytown'…dealing with a bit of debt and a bit of divorce, conveyancing and all of a sudden he's got to deal with this stuff…And you get someone like a sharp solicitor or barrister, they're nervous and they're giving possession."*

Notwithstanding these criticisms, there was also praise for some judges in their sensitivity, thoroughness and reasonableness in their approach. One senior officer commented:

> *"They are generally speaking as a body, very very impressive…there are a number of judgements that we have seen that have been, I think, magnificent. I mean the grasp of the six day trial, the analysis of the evidence, the judgement of the veracity of the individuals who have presented evidence to the court, all of them detailed in a judgement, is a very impressive thing to behold."*

In general, respondents perceived judges to be sympathetic and understanding toward landlords, although some felt that sometimes they were inclined to favour the defendant tenant. As one officer put it:

> *"I feel that generally judges are for the underdog, you know, and they give them every lee way before they will evict anybody. And I suppose that's fair 'cos it's a big decision to throw somebody out of their home."*

Some thought there had been changes in judges' approach since the 1996 Act. The effect of the heightened media profile of anti-social behaviour along with the increased preparation of the cases coming before judges made them take the cases more seriously.

Given the discretion given to judges in this area it is likely that different judges will have different approaches, although further training might lead to greater consistency, and certainly greater familiarity with the law. It was felt generally that the judiciary needed to be more familiar with the problems in a particular locality and should adopt Lord Woolf's (Woolf, 1996) recommendation to visit estates and talk to residents.

❏ Defence lawyers and Legal Aid

The defendants' case stories illustrate the difficulties they experienced in finding someone who could represent them properly. Interviews with landlords and defence lawyers confirmed that in many areas there appeared to be only a small number of committed housing lawyers who were able to act for defendants in anti-social behaviour cases. In some of our case study areas we found it impossible to identify any legal firm which was regularly active in this area of work. Landlords' lawyers reported that on occasions defence lawyers really did not have adequate knowledge of housing law and invariably lost the case for the client. Examples were also found of where defendants had been badly advised and where lawyers had advised them to drop the case because of a failure to obtain Legal Aid. The research seemed to indicate that defendants were often very poorly served.

Where there were lawyers who were prepared and more experienced in these kinds of cases, they all faced the problem of obtaining Legal Aid. It was reported that it was particularly difficult to get Legal Aid where the landlord had established a ground for possession, but defence lawyers thought it was important to challenge the 'reasonableness' of such an action (see above). As one para-legal put it,

> *"In my view, every tenant who gets served with a summons, deserves representation, and deserves at least a fighting cause to try and keep them in their home, because even if the grounds for possession is met, and in this case it's nuisance and annoyance, the court still has to be satisfied that it is reasonable in all the circumstances."*

The ability to obtain Legal Aid varied enormously from one area to another. Examples were given of no problem occurring in one area, but in another, 50 miles away, obtaining Legal Aid was described as a nightmare. Most of those spoken to said that they had managed to get Legal Aid in the end, but not without a very hard struggle at every stage in the case. One lawyer found that he always had to go to appeal to get Legal Aid granted. Another lawyer complained bitterly about the difficulties created by the interpretation of the rules by his local Legal Aid Board around getting Legal Aid for injunctions. Even where defendants were willing to give undertakings, which the board required, landlords were very reluctant to accept undertakings, so defendants could be placed in a Catch 22 position. Another defence lawyer found that the Legal Aid Board penalised them if the defendant refused to give an undertaking because they did not want to admit they were at fault. Another thought success in obtaining Legal Aid depended on willingness to negotiate with landlords at every stage pre-trial, ultimately trying to prevent the case actually going to court, thus reducing potential costs for the Legal Aid Board.

The difficulties of obtaining Legal Aid, and the conditions made at different stages of the case, invariably resulted in delays in getting the case to court. One very experienced private solicitor was of the opinion that pressure could be brought to bear upon the Legal Aid Board once a trial date had been set. The effect of obtaining Legal Aid was illustrated by one private solicitor who commented that they might drop a case if they found out that the defendant had got Legal Aid and was going to defend, *"to the hilt"*, because of the extra costs that would be incurred through a longer trial.

Without exception, defence lawyers stated that defendants should have easier access to Legal Aid, with appropriately experienced lawyers. The development of the Community Legal Service may address some of these issues. The service, which was launched in April 2000:

> *"aims to provide a comprehensive and accessible network of quality legal service provides with special emphasis on addressing local needs"* (Legal Aid Board Franchise Development Group, 2000).

Summary

Contrary to landlords' perception that courts were unwilling to grant possession orders, an outright order was found to be the most likely outcome to possession action. It is clear that in cases involving extremely disturbing anti-social behaviour, the granting of such orders could resolve major management problems on estates and ensure more efficient use of resource.

As an alternative to possession action, landlords can use injunctions. This remedy has the advantage of enabling action to be taken without the threat of eviction and the possible displacement of the problem. Surprisingly, despite recent amendments strengthening the power of injunctions, very few landlords could provide any information about their use. While just under two-thirds of local authorities stated they were prepared to use injunctions an examination of action taken in individual cases showed that in practice they were rarely employed. The small number of organisations who regularly used injunctions were very positive about their benefits. But, frequently, landlords lacked the necessary knowledge or skills to use them.

Most landlords were positive about their relationships with the courts and judges, although concerns did emerge about delay, the intimidatory atmosphere of courts and inconsistent decision making from judges. In some areas it was clear that defendants did not have access to proper legal services to defend claims.

CHAPTER 10

TENANTS' EXPERIENCES

The scrutiny of the defendant case file survey enabled a detailed examination of action taken by landlords in individual cases to be undertaken. In addition, interviews with tenants[1] – both complainants and defendants – provided evidence of their views on the effectiveness of legal action to deal with neighbour nuisance. The experiences reported by complainants and defendants were in most part traumatic and in some cases quite tragic.

Neither the complainants nor defendants interviewed were drawn from a random sample but were selected either by the case study landlords or by an independent para-legal advisor. The researchers are aware that these cases may not be typical of all anti-social behaviour cases. In selecting the complainants, (8) to be interviewed, landlords tended to refer to cases where there had been prolonged and serious problems, and thus it is likely that the nature of the problems portrayed in the case study sample were more extreme than that found in many anti-social behaviour cases. Unfortunately, it was impossible to obtain interviews with the perpetrators involved in the cases reported by complainants. However, contact was made with a small number of defendants (6), who were prepared to tell their stories. These cases can also not be seen to be representative of defendants in general, since most of the cases were chosen by an independent legal advisor specialising in defence work, and were restricted to cases where the legal advisor felt that inappropriate legal action had been taken, and where the legal outcome had resulted in the case being dismissed, withdrawn or a suspended possession order being awarded. It is unclear to the researchers whether these cases solely represent isolated incidences or whether they are illustrative of a wider

---

1. With the exception of one case, which involved owner-occupiers living next door to council tenants, all the complainants and defendants interviewed were tenants of social landlords.

problem for social landlords, although given the number of similar cases drawn to our attention since completing the interviews we feel they are likely to be symptomatic of problems which can occur. In either event, these defendants had a different story to tell than the one popularly characterised in the media as, 'nightmare neighbours.'

❏ The complainants' perspective

The eight complainants interviewed were drawn from a range of household types (see Appendix 1). The problems that they initially endured were in the main associated with noise nuisance, albeit from different sources, with the problems subsequently escalating to incorporate abuse, harassment, and even physical assault. By the time of the interviews, most complainants had achieved some sort of resolution to their problems, and had had time to reflect on their experiences. Without exception, they all expressed the view that they had suffered prolonged periods of stress as a result of the behaviour of their neighbours and that the issue had dominated their lives. While each of the complainants' stories was unique, a number of common features emerged from the analysis of complainants' views of the use of legal remedies to deal with anti-social behaviour. The majority of complainants did not feel positive about the way they had been treated by their landlord. In particular complainants criticised landlords for:

- Delays in taking appropriate action.

- Lack of adequate support from front line officers and the importance of specialist units/officers.

- Failure to protect them from witness intimidation and the negative experience of going to court.

Delays in taking appropriate action

A common feature of the complainants' reports concerned criticisms of the length of time it had taken for landlords to take action. Many reported that they were forced to live with the consequences of the anti-social behaviour for some time, with little or no action being taken by their landlord. Some stated that they had experienced great difficulty in getting the landlord to take their complaints seriously. Mr. and Mrs. Brown's experience is typical, in so far as it demonstrates how delays in taking appropriate action can exacerbate the problems experienced by complainants.

Mr. and Mrs. Brown

Mr. and Mrs. Brown and their two teenage children had been council tenants for over 16 years. For four years, they suffered from verbal abuse, noise, and violent and threatening behaviour from their immediate neighbours, a couple with young children. As soon as the trouble started, Mr. Brown contacted his landlord, however, he felt initially that the local housing officer did not believe him and it took two and a half years before his landlord took his complaints seriously. Warnings were issued to the neighbours and Mr. Brown was asked to keep daily log sheets of incidents. Eventually the landlord commenced possession proceedings and Mr. Brown agreed to give evidence in court.

"As you can imagine, I was very, very apprehensive, very apprehensive about giving evidence against them. But, you know, I finally come to the decision, if this is the only way I'm going to get some type of redress or some stability put back in my life, I'm going to do it."

Further problems occurred during the period leading up to the possession hearing when, on three occasions, the case was adjourned. Mr. Brown described the effect these delays had on his wife.

"On one occasion, twenty four hours before I was due to go to court, I received a phone call from [the authority]. 'Mr. Brown I don't know how you're going to take this.' And my heart sank; I knew what she was going to say. My wife just looked at me…she just broke down crying, because we had been under that much pressure."

The problem was only finally resolved when the landlord transferred the neighbours to alternative accommodation.

As a result of his experience, Mr. Brown felt that justice had not been done and wondered how their neighbours had managed to avoid having any sanctions imposed on them as a result of their disruptive and aggressive behaviour.

Lack of adequate support from the landlord and the importance of specialist units/officers

A further common criticism voiced by complainants focussed on landlords' failure to provide them with adequate support. Many of those interviewed reported that they had made persistent approaches to their landlord in order to obtain adequate support. The complainants felt that landlords tended not to appreciate the degree of torment they had experienced and the courage it took to be a witness in an anti-social behaviour case. In one case it took six years of regular diary keeping and other methods of evidence collection and involved reporting severe and occasionally violent and threatening behaviour, before decisive action was taken. Some tenants had been made ill by the landlord's apparent lack of action.

The following case study illustrates the feelings expressed by many complainants about how their landlord had failed to provide them with appropriate help and support.

Rachel

Rachel's problems with her next door neighbour started with a long held family grievance. Her neighbour's behaviour quickly deteriorated to include harassment, intimidation, and violence. As the situation escalated Rachel contacted her landlord who suggested she approach the neighbours to try to resolve the problems. Rachel felt the landlord did not want to get involved:

> "They tended to make you feel a little bit like…'Isn't there something that you could have perhaps done to have prevented this from happening? We don't like this problem, it's not good for us.' And really that's the last thing that you want to hear."

After further incidents, the police took criminal action under the Protection from Harassment Act 1997, which resulted in the neighbour's partner being given a custodial sentence and the neighbour receiving a suspended sentence and restraining order. During the criminal proceedings, Rachel said she had received no support from her landlord and was told that a letter from them could make the situation worse. Rachel felt that her landlord's response only became more positive with the employment of a new housing officer:

> "Since Ms Smith was involved in this case I cannot fault her in any way, shape or form. She moved everything her powers could and more…They were fantastic. But I think sometimes, that the right people don't do the right jobs, and I think it took a special person to make all this happen and she did. She was not gonna let these people do this to us."

Eventually the landlord took possession proceedings and an outright order was granted. For Rachel the whole experience was very traumatic and resulted in her needing stress counselling.

The quality, commitment and skills of housing officers to respond to incidents of anti-social behaviour appeared to vary both between organisations and within organisations. As in Rachel's case, it was reported by many complainants that a change in personnel was an important catalyst in changing the landlord's approach. If an experienced, specialist or committed officer was attached to the case, then much more confidence was transmitted to complainants that appropriate action would be forthcoming. The best evidence of overall support came from tenants of landlords who had access to specialist units or officers, as Mr. and Mrs. Green's case illustrates.

Mr. and Mrs. Green (owner-occupiers)

Mr. and Mrs. Green, a couple with three young children lived next door to council tenants who started to behave in an abusive, threatening and a violent manner towards the Greens. The trouble originated within three weeks of the perpetrators moving in, with a threat to kill Mr. Green. Subsequently the neighbours' children's caused incessant vandalism to the Green's garden. There were also incidents of domestic violence within the perpetrator's family as well as a lack of parental care over the children, with the toddlers often found wandering down the main road unattended, and the older ones throwing objects at passing cars.

Despite the severity of the problems, the Greens reported that they had to spend six years filling in diary reports before the landlord took their case seriously. Mr. Green described his sense of powerlessness and the futility he felt maintaining records of incidences when no action was taken:

"I mean in the end you would just fill out, with the paper, you'd think: 'I'm sick of this', and you'd take them round. I mean, you were supposed to take them round every couple of weeks or every week, or whatever, these sheets. But you get so...you come in from work and the first thing you do is get abuse, it's like 'Oh, not again'. And you've got to try and get on with, I mean, I don't think they realise...They say, 'jot everything down...what happens'. "

The Greens felt the landlord's approach changed only when a specialist Neighbour Nuisance Officer was appointed who collected extensive evidence, including detailed witness statements and video surveillance. 11 months and three court hearings later, an outright possession order was granted against the perpetrators. Despite the support of the specialist officer, Mr. and Mrs. Green found the experience of giving formal evidence in court very frightening and intimidating due to the proximity of the defendants.

The risk of witness intimidation and the negative experience of going to court

Despite a general perception from housing and legal officers that the majority of intimidation experienced by tenants concerned the fear of, rather than actual, intimidation, for most of the case study complainants the intimidation experienced was real enough. In the majority of cases, the complainants interviewed were the only people prepared to act as witnesses, as other neighbours were reported as being too frightened. This fear appeared to be well founded since all the complainants reported that the scale of the anti-social behaviour intensified if the alleged perpetrators found out who had complained about them.

In some cases where the complainants identity was revealed (sometimes as a result of warning letters issued by the landlord) physical retaliation and intimidation occurred. The types of intimidation experienced included a catalogue of harassment, threats of violence, threats to kill a child, pets killed, damage to property and abusive verbal attacks. In one extreme example the complainants were set upon in their own home by a gang of the perpetrator's relatives and were attacked and beaten for 20 minutes. In addition to harassment and intimidation from the alleged perpetrators, all of those who had acted as witnesses for the landlord found the experience of giving formal evidence in court stressful, describing it variously as, "horrible", "terrible" and "petrifying."

The following case exemplifies the types of intimidation and harassment that can affect complainants.

Mrs. White and Jean Gray

For Mrs. White and her friend Jean Gray, who had been council tenants for many years, the trouble originated with three families living in the neighbourhood. Gangs of young people engaged in late night socialising, drug abuse, theft and vandalism. When Mrs White and Jean first complained to their landlord about this disruptive behaviour they felt their complaints were, *"shoved under the carpet."* Eventually, however, the specialist Neighbour Nuisance Team provided support by the installation of panic buttons and video surveillance.

→

When possession proceedings were started, the anti-social behaviour escalated and both Mrs. White and Jean were subject to extreme intimidation and harassment, including the killing of a kitten, threats to fire bomb their houses and harm their children. Jean explained how traumatic the experience was:

> *"People don't know what you have to go through. All right to say 'do a statement and we'll have 'em in a few months.' But that few months waiting to go to court has put us through hell."*

Jean and Mrs. White attended six court hearings to give evidence of repeated breaches of interim injunctions before an outright possession order was granted. They found the experience terrifying, particularly given the number of defendants in court, as Jean explained,

> *"you've got one at the back like this [hitting his palm with his fist in a threatening manner] with his fist. Well, the housing manager, he had his hands on the thing giving his statement, and he was shaking, wasn't he?"*

Jean became ill as a result of the stress of the case and had to take four months off work. But despite the extreme intimidation and harassment experienced by both of the complainants, they both felt that they would be prepared to take the same action again if necessary, and they are now starting up a residents' association.

❏ The defendants' experience

As with the complainants, the defendants interviewed were drawn from a range of household types (see Appendix 1). Although the defendant sample bias meant that such cases could not be regarded as typical of all anti-social behaviour cases, it is interesting to note that in many respects the economic and social profile of the defendants interviewed was very similar to the defendant profile found in the larger case file survey (see Chapter 2).

In common with the analysis of complainants' experience, analysis of defendants' experiences revealed a number of common criticisms regarding landlord's actions to resolve the nuisance which are examined in more detail below:

- lack of rigorous investigation of complaints;
- inadequate evidence collection methods employed;
- inappropriate action being taken and a failure to involve other agencies.

Lack of rigorous investigation of complaints

A frequent criticism by defendants concerned the lack of rigorous investigation of complaints by landlords. In four of the six cases, defendants claimed that the landlord had made no direct contact with them before commencing legal action. In the remaining two cases the defendants felt that the housing officer(s) concerned was only prepared to listen to the complainant's side of the argument, not engaging in any independent investigation or even asking the defendants about their perspective. In neighbour nuisance cases it can be notoriously difficult to establish precisely which household is at fault. This was also illustrated by one of the case files where the landlord had been unable to resolve the situation and the officer had noted on file: *"I'm really unsure what to do here…the situation can't go on, but I don't know who to believe."*

Without adequate investigations it is impossible to make an informed decision as to the most appropriate form of action for the landlord to take. The following case illustrates the need for landlords to ensure that thorough investigations are undertaken prior to making the decision to take legal action.

Peter and Gail

Peter and Gail, a couple in their early forties, had to all accounts been model tenants for the previous eight years. Gail suffered from ill health including multiple sclerosis, angina, partial deafness and psychiatric problems. Their problems began when they transferred from a large city to a small development in a different town. The day they moved into their new home, their neighbours, who had purchased their house under the Right to Buy provisions, started to complain about noise nuisance.

Three days later when interviewed by a housing officer, Peter and Gail felt they were not given a chance to put their side of the story:

> *"She dismissed us fully…right out of hand. She kept saying to us, she knew this woman for a lot of years…and she was 100 per cent behind her…She never investigated it, believe me, she never investigated it."*

→

Following further complaints involving the police, the landlord started proceedings for possession on the grounds of noise nuisance. In a witness statement the landlord claimed that mediation had been offered. This offer was disputed by Gail and Peter and because they were new to the area they found it very difficult to get support from other agencies.

Four or five neighbours attended the possession hearing to give evidence on Peter and Gail's behalf and the case was withdrawn. One year later, at the time of the interview, the complainants had sold their house and no further complaints had been received about Gail and Peter.

Both Peter and Gail felt that they had been treated unfairly, and were disillusioned with the courts, the police and their landlord.

> *"We were set up, from day one....First and foremost, I think the housing officer should have done her job. I know it's in the policies and all that, her job should have been to find out both sides. What happened here, whatever reason she's got, there were no two sides. It was one side and from this day on I'll still say: 'Why did they pick on us and why didn't they want us to have this property, I do not know'..."*

Reliance solely on criminal prosecutions

One aspect of failure to investigate properly highlighted by defence lawyers, concerned cases where eviction was sought solely on the ground of a previous criminal conviction.

Interviews with defendants provided evidence that in some instances the decision to take eviction action was based solely on this ground, without any further investigation into the history of the matter, or its impact on neighbours. Although conviction for an arrestable offence, in, or in the locality of, the premises and/or use of the dwelling for activities which are illegal or immoral constitutes grounds for possession, landlords must also provide evidence to the court that such action would be reasonable. In the following cases, possession action was commenced some considerable time after the defendants had been convicted of criminal offences and in each case it appeared that the landlord had failed to consider the question of 'reasonableness'.

John Smith

John who was in his early 50s and his wife, had been council tenants for over 24 years. They had two children, a son of 21, and a daughter aged 18, who had learning difficulties. Following a serious burn injury, John became addicted to Temazepan and was subsequently convicted of possessing and supplying the drug. Two years after the original offence, possession action was commenced on the grounds that John had been convicted of an arrestable offence. The first Notice of Seeking Possession was issued to John in prison while he was half way through a two year custodial sentence. Subsequently a complaint was made about his daughters' behaviour and a second NSP was also served.

Both notices were served by post and no attempt was made by the landlord to contact John or his family. In court the housing officer responsible acknowledged his failure to visit the family. John recounted what was said in court:

> "The council were wrong all the way through it. They admitted in court they were wrong, the housing manager didn't have a leg to stand on. Every time my barrister said to him like, 'Should you have?' he said, 'In hindsight, I should have.' That's the only thing he could say…It was all what they should have done but they never done. No-one from the council came near us at all. It was hard but, like I say, no-one from the council seemed to care about that you know, it's just a case of, 'we're going to get you out and you know we don't care'…"

In John's view the problem was caused by the housing officer's lack of experience:

> "He was a young lad and he was really out of his depth because you could see in his face that he hadn't got the slightest idea really of what he was talking about."

John found the experience of being taken to court very stressful but at the possession hearing was supported by 12 of his immediate neighbours who gave evidence in his defence. A suspended possession order was made but John thought this could have been avoided if the authority had made greater efforts to investigate his case.

Mary and Ben and their 25 year old daughter, Jane

Mary and Ben, an elderly couple, had been council tenants for over 30 years with no previous history of anti-social behaviour. Their daughter, Jane, a heroin addict and a single parent with a 5 year old son, lived in the same street. Following a police visit to Mary's house, in connection with Jane's use of drugs, both Mary and Jane were convicted for conspiracy to handle stolen goods. Mary was given a custodial sentence and Jane a probation order on condition that she attend a rehabilitation unit. At the time of the convictions the landlord made no contact with Mary or Jane, but two years later and nine months after Mary had completed her custodial sentence, they were both served with Notices of Seeking Possession followed by a possession summons.

On seeking legal advice their solicitor took statements from neighbours and professionals, which resulted in their cases being withdrawn due to lack of evidence. The effect of the possession action was devastating for both families. Following the criminal conviction Jane had stopped using heroin and had been 'clean' for nine months but following the NSP she lapsed back into her addiction. In Mary's view their landlord had not considered all the circumstances prior to taking legal action:

"I think they should be made to behave differently, because they are killing you off really."

Inappropriate action being taken and a failure to involve other agencies

The lack of training given to many housing officers combined with the pressure of other management tasks may be factors which contributed to officers taking an insensitive and occasionally heavy handed approach in some anti-social behaviour cases (see Chapter 7). In the following example it appeared that the problems arose in part from initial allocation of an unsuitable property, followed by a lack of investigation into all the circumstances. In this case the actions of the landlord and their legal advisor appeared ill considered and were the subject of a reprimand from the appeal judge.

Anne

Following an argument with her parents, Anne, a teenager, was nominated for a housing association flat. The flat was situated on the first floor in a block occupied predominantly by elderly people. Although the existing residents petitioned the landlord not to go ahead with the allocation Anne was granted the tenancy. Complaints about noise nuisance started the day she moved in: *"There was a knock on the door asking me to wear slippers when I walked around and to buy earphones to watch the television."* Three days after Anne moved the landlord sent a hand delivered letter in which they asked her to consider terminating her tenancy. Two days later she received a further letter telling her that an expedited court hearing for immediate possession was to be sought. At the possession hearing, held only two weeks after Anne had moved into the property, an outright possession order was granted (see Chapter 9 for details of the court proceedings).

Anne subsequently obtained legal advice and lodged an appeal. At the appeal hearing the judge criticised the way the case had been managed. He stated that what had occurred was: *"a wholly unreasonable exercise of discretion, a breach of natural justice and plainly wrong."* The appeal judge asked the landlord to consider transferring Anne to alternative accommodation. This option was declined and in the end Anne was offered accommodation by the local authority.

During the possession process Anne was supported by a youth worker who expressed the view that the problem was caused by Anne being given inappropriate accommodation. In addition to the clash of life styles between Anne and her elderly neighbours, the building had insufficient soundproofing and as Anne had no furniture or carpeting, complaints were inevitable. Anne felt that when the problems started the landlord should have talked to her about the complaints and considered transferring her to alternative accommodation.

❏ Summary

The analysis of the complainants' and defendants' experiences illustrates the complexity of the nature of neighbour nuisance. Anti-social behaviour can be extremely serious and disruptive, destroying the quality of life of all the people affected by it. In every case, housing officers need to interview both complainant(s) and the alleged perpetrator(s) in order to exercise a professional judgement as to the most appropriate action to take. It is clear that the complainants interviewed endured prolonged periods of anxiety and stress whilst seeking a resolution of the problems. Acting as witnesses for landlords in injunction or possession proceedings required great courage. In some of the cases, there was evidence that landlords were taking the issue very seriously and were developing appropriate specialist skills and knowledge including the employment of specialist officers or teams of officers to deal with serious anti-social behaviour cases. However, all too often complainants were disappointed by the landlord's response and thought that more effective action could have been taken at an earlier stage.

Equally, analysis of the case study defendants' experiences underlines the importance of housing officers adopting an impartial approach when investigating complaints. The study findings indicate the need for specialist training of officers to enable them to act in a professional manner when confronted with conflicting accounts of events. The interviews with housing officers, their legal advisors and indeed defendants and complainants all highlight the need for landlords to ensure that housing officers have the skills, knowledge and resources to be able to undertake thorough investigations, collect and evaluate detailed evidence, and provide adequate witness support in individual cases. Without such specialist skills there is a danger that inappropriate action many be taken causing distress and frustration to all involved.

CHAPTER 11

LEGAL COSTS

The survey data showed that generally landlords had very little idea about the costs involved in taking legal action. Just over a third of registered social landlords (37 per cent) and only two out of ten (21 per cent) local authorities stated that they could estimate the costs of legal proceedings taken during 1997/98. Whilst it can be difficult accurately to estimate costs in cases that are subject to ongoing action over a long period of time, it is likely that organisations' inability to identify costs also reflected their lack of effective recording and monitoring procedures (see Chapter 3).

Chart 9: Ability to estimate legal costs by local authority type in 1997/98

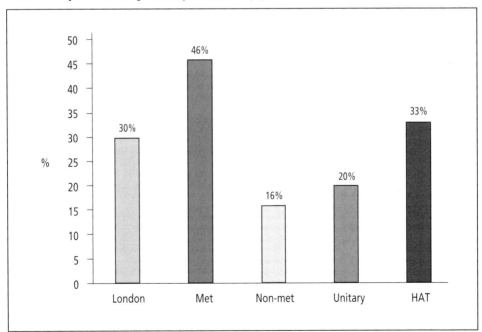

Number of respondents: *London=10; Metropolitan=13; Non-metropolitan=83; Unitary=20; HAT=3*

The larger nationally based registered social landlords and small authorities were least likely to be able to estimate costs, with nearly nine out of ten (90 per cent LAs, 88 per cent RSLs) unable to do so. Conversely, four out of ten of the larger authorities (those managing more than 15,000 properties) and over half (57 per cent) of the smallest registered social landlords (those managing less than 1,500 properties) were able to provide estimates of the cost of legal action. Chart 9 shows that the differences in local authorities' ability to estimate costs were related to the type of authority, with metropolitan authorities and London boroughs more likely to provide this information than non-metropolitan and unitary authorities.

Where organisations could provide details of the costs associated with litigation, differences between registered social landlords and authorities emerged. Generally, local authorities' estimated costs were reported as being more than twice as high as costs identified by registered social landlords. The median cost of taking legal action for authorities was £10,400 with an associated range of between £142 and £305,338, whilst the median cost reported by registered social landlords was less than half this figure, at £4,000, with a range of between £500 and £80,000. This may reflect the fact that those authorities able to provide estimates were taking more action than those registered social landlords, rather than the fact that authorities' costs were higher on a per case basis.

Interviews with the case study landlords confirmed that most could not give any details of the overall costs involved in taking legal action. Many officers stated they had no idea and could not even give an estimate. Even where some information could be provided, the estimates varied widely. For example, a local authority solicitor estimated legal costs for an undefended possession action to be as little as £500, which when taken with an estimate of the cost of officer time gave a total of £1,000-£1,500. Average costs quoted by other landlords tended to be much higher than this with the costs for possession estimated to be in the region of £3,000. In general, local authority solicitors tended to cite cheaper rates than private solicitors. For example, a private solicitor cited £4000-£5,000 as the average cost for possession with costs rising with the number of witnesses, his most expensive being £10,000 for a two to three day trial. Another private solicitor cited his most expensive case as £45,000 for eight days in court. An undefended case was estimated by two organisations as being around £1,000. The high cost of using a professional witness was illustrated by one organisation who cited they added an extra £5,000-7,000 to the cost of a case.

Injunction action was generally estimated to cost less than possession action, with the average cited for injunctions being in the region of £1,000. However, again there were significant variations in landlords' estimates. Two local authority lawyers cited £500, whilst one private solicitor cited £600-700, with another estimating the cost to be £2,000. It was not always clear if the costs quoted included barristers' fees or not. Where these fees were explicitly included one local authority solicitor cited a minimum of £2,000-£3,000 for a successful defended case.

Previous research (Dignan *et al.*, 1996, pp 77-79) has managed to give some indication of the true cost (at 1995/96 prices) of housing officer time and indirect costs incurred through lost revenue and increased expenditure in repairs and allocation processes. This study also highlighted the extreme complexity of working out the true financial cost of anti-social behaviour cases, whether it involved preventative and ameliorative work, or whether it meant taking the case through the legal process. Not only are there the costs of housing officer time and the stresses incurred through managing a bigger caseload, but there are also many other quantifiable as well as unquantifiable costs incurred.

The case study landlords found it virtually impossible to estimate the cost in housing officer time, and for some this was not even something that was thought about. Generally, however, it was recognised that cases were very resource intensive. One local authority officer guesstimated that in their large authority the costs in officer time must be millions of pounds a year, but it was very difficult to find ways to measure such costs accurately. A few officers commented that this lack of knowledge would not inhibit the taking of that action since the non-legal costs were usually absorbed within the housing management budget.

TEST, which provided an evidence collection service for registered social landlords, charged a flat fee of £400 per case prior to legal action. However this fee structure was in the process of being revised since it was felt that it did not reflect the true costs. In addition, the use of a flat rate fee was thought to be an incentive for landlords to refer their most difficult cases. As a result of these problems TEST had undertaken an analysis of the costs of collecting evidence and were confident that their charges were less than the costs of using front line housing officers.

❏ **Summary**

Until landlords improve their recording and monitoring of cases, it is in effect impossible to quantify the exact costs of differing forms of action to deal with anti-social behaviour. Despite the lack of any hard data, landlords were clear that anti-social behaviour cases were resource intensive and made significant inroads into their housing management budgets.

CHAPTER 12

INTRODUCTORY AND STARTER TENANCIES

The development of 12 month introductory tenancies, without security of tenure, created much controversy when first introduced in 1996. Such tenancies were seen as the first steps to undermine tenants' rights since the introduction of the Tenants' Charter in 1980. Some commentators even suggested that they, *"represent the beginning of the end of the security of tenure for local housing authority tenants"* (Smith and George, 1997).

Introductory tenancies cannot be used by registered social landlords. Some registered social landlords have, however, developed an equivalent to the introductory tenancy by using assured shorthold (starter) tenancies. The use of such tenancies is strictly regulated by the Housing Corporation who will only permit a RSL to use assured shorthold tenancies if, *"steps are needed to prevent or reverse social conditions in an area threatening the housing rights of most residents or the value of the stock."* (Housing Corporation, 1998, p 45)

The survey indicated that there were far fewer registered social landlords (13 per cent) operating such tenancies than local authorities (30 per cent), although it appeared that registered social landlords were more likely to be thinking about using them in the future. A further 14 per cent of registered social landlords were intending to adopt their use compared with a further 7 per cent of authorities. There were distinct variations in their use, with non-metropolitan authorities being half as likely as other authorities to adopt them. Of the case study areas three out of four of the authorities used them, while four of the registered social landlords had some (limited) experience.

❏ **Effectiveness**

There were mixed responses regarding their effectiveness. For many, they had been in place for too short a time to gauge with much confidence whether they made a long-term effect on tenants' behaviour. One officer thought that a well worded tenancy agreement followed up by clear action was a better approach. While they worked by helping to make it clear to tenants the landlord's approach to dealing with anti-social behaviour, many officers from both types of landlord thought that they should be seen as part of a wider package of measures to prevent and control anti-social behaviour, and that on their own they might not be very effective

Often they were introduced with the backing of tenants' representatives and as a result of tenant pressure. One local authority front line officer said:

> *"We had about two or three thousand responses, saying what a brilliant idea. Most of them saying, 'wonderful', 'not before time', comments like that. I think we had about 14 people who actually said they were maybe a bad idea."*

Some officers reported they had resulted in larger caseloads for already hard pressed housing officers, with extra visiting and work necessary to undertake a review before deciding whether to terminate the tenancy. There were also concerns about the procedure around termination of these kinds of tenancies, with officers not being trained for this role, of tenants being open to vindictiveness and malicious complaints by other tenants, and having high and wrong expectations of the landlord being able to evict 'at a sneeze'. One defence lawyer illustrated some of these concerns:

> *"I've come across some housing officers who can only be described as racist, bigoted, prejudiced, biased. And you are asking these people to determine security of tenure?...I don't think the landlord, or an employee of the landlord should determine whether my client or tenant should be evicted or not. They've got a vested interest. It may be that there's a big waiting list for a property and they want to rehouse someone for that property."*

Responses showed some confusion around the eviction process and standards of proof required. The review process was seen as not necessarily as exacting as if conducted in a court of law, which was perturbing for some officers. One front line officer, however, thought the shorter review process, compared with the lengthy court procedure, was a real asset. Even amongst solicitors there was a difference of opinion. As one put it, you, *"didn't have to call any evidence"*, while another was adamant that the landlord had to act *"reasonably"*. One senior local authority officer thought introductory tenancies had helped in getting evictions for some anti-social behaviour cases because less evidence was needed.

> *"And in those cases we would have definitely had a problem in getting witnesses willing to go to court. And maybe based on our experience with the county courts, the amount of evidence that was available would not have convinced the court to give us a possession order. But in the cases that we have prepared as introductory tenancies we've felt that it was justified. The review panel of councillors have examined the thing and they've felt it was justified. So we've been able to deal with four quite serious cases of anti-social behaviour and prevent them from becoming secure tenants."*

Officers were also very aware of the power that they were exerting over individuals' lives, and this required them to be very rigorous in their own evidence collection and judgement.

> *"But because of the review hearing process, and our review is a panel of local councillors, we have to get it right and the detail of the work has got to be done much much more precisely than it was done in the past. Because you're making the decision aren't you. You know you're making the decision whereas in the past it's the court makes the decision based on the evidence, you've got a longer time to put it together…"*

Evidence from the survey indicated that the majority of evictions from introductory tenancies were for rent arrears (68 per cent) and only 19 per cent were for neighbour nuisance. One defence lawyer was particularly scathing about the way introductory tenancies were not being used for their original purpose. Although they were being used to evict tenants for anti-social behaviour problems, they were also being used to evict for minor rent arrears, and this was seen as an abuse of power and inappropriate.

Officers of a registered social landlord operating in an area suffering major problems with low demand, showed concern about the message sent out by adopting starter tenancies and their contribution to an already large transient population who don't stay for much longer than 12 months anyway. Here there was a need for a more strategic multi-agency approach along with sifting out problems at the application stage. Concern was also expressed about the creation of further stigma with an estate that might be singled out for starter tenancies, and that if they were to adopt them then it should be applied consistently across all tenancies.

Many of these issues also emerged from a Housing Corporation study of starter and introductory tenancies (Ruggieri and Levison, 1998), although they concluded that starter tenancies have been successful in sending a message out to new and existing tenants that anti-social behaviour will not be tolerated, and that combined with other regeneration schemes for the area, they could attract more stable communities.

❏ Summary

At the time of the survey, just under a third of local authorities had adopted introductory tenancies, with a further one in ten planning to introduce them in the next 12 months. This compared to one in ten registered social landlords using starter tenancies, and just under one in five planning to adopt them in the next 12 months. Distinct regional variations in the use of temporary tenancies were noted.

Nearly half of the landlords using introductory tenancies had subsequently evicted tenants. How far the use of introductory tenancies can be seen, as a tool being used against anti-social tenants must, however, be doubted since most cases for eviction were for rent arrears. Landlords also expressed many concerns over their effectiveness, with landlords operating in areas of low demand particularly sceptical.

CHAPTER 13

DISPLACEMENT AND EXCLUSION

❏ Displacement of the problem to other housing sectors

In taking legal action to deal with anti-social behaviour, front line officers, in particular, were aware of potential problems that could arise when households are evicted, abandon or are excluded from social housing tenancies. Officers were concerned about the long-term effectiveness of possession action:

> *"And in some cases it's solved the problem, but in others it doesn't because they just move to another address within the community. There's two notable cases I can think of where we've got a possession order, they've been evicted and they've moved to an adjacent street."*

While one officer expressed the view that as long as the nuisance perpetrator moved from the estate she was responsible for, she didn't care where they went, more commonly officers *were* concerned about use of eviction action, particularly if families were involved. A number of respondents commented on the ongoing problems that can occur when perpetrators move into the private sector or with other social landlords. With the increased diversity of providers operating in social housing estates, including the legacy of Right to Buy properties, it is not uncommon for households who have been evicted to seek tenancies in the same locality. Thus, despite regaining possession, the nuisance behaviour may continue with the landlord having little control over further enforcement action to stop the offending behaviour with a resulting loss of confidence by the local community in the landlord.

In order to tackle such problems, a number of proposals were made, some of which had recognised problems and drawbacks, many to do with data protection.

··

Proposals to deal with the displacement of the problem to the private sector

- Strategies to recognise that social landlords are operating within a competitive environment with alternative accommodation available in many social housing estates.
- The development of closer working relationships with private sector providers. This was felt to be increasingly important also in the light of provisions in the Crime and Disorder Act for consideration of *all* residents.
- Private sector landlords brought into the ambit of regulations that social sector landlords abide by; private sector landlords ought to be able to buy into their systems, and become part of a wider joint agency approach. Confidentiality was seen as more problematic here.
- Greater local authority powers to licence private sector landlords and to have some input into the rehousing of households who are evicted or excluded from social housing as a result of neighbour nuisance.
- Improved flows of information in anti-social behaviour cases between estate managers and landlords operating in a particular locality.

··

❑ Exclusion policies

Linked to the problems that can arise when households with a history of anti-social behaviour move into the private sector is the impact of the growing trend for social landlords to operate formal or informal exclusion policies. In the survey, 46 per cent of registered social landlords had one, compared with 52 per cent of local authorities, and like introductory tenancies, metropolitan authorities were almost twice as likely (86 per cent) to have one, compared to non-metropolitan authorities (45 per cent). Those in our case studies, which did, had generally only operated an official one in the last year or so, although others had been operating one unofficially for some time before. As one front line housing officer commented:

> *"There's no exclusion list. But there are characters that have appeared before, that you've had renting your properties and have left and re-applied, that you wouldn't touch with a barge-pole."*

Criteria for exclusion varied, with one registered social landlord saying that they would exclude if there had been a history of complaints even though there had not been any court action or eviction, whereas others would be quite flexible, with a couple of others excluding only where there was proof that tenants had been guilty of breaching their tenancy within the last two years, or established evidence of serious anti-social behaviour or where an order had been made. Another would exclude if tenants were suspected of not being able to abide by the tenancy agreement. One authority felt an explicit exclusion policy was unnecessary since the decision was effectively made through the homelessness decision making process, the route through which the majority of allocations were made.

The time limit on exclusion also varied. While many seemed to indicate that they were relatively flexible about when they would reconsider someone, others in reality would effectively be permanently excluded, having refused all appeals. Another case study local authority would reconsider after between three and five years if the applicant could demonstrate there had been no further incidents of anti-social behaviour within that time. In one local authority the tough line on permanent exclusions promoted by councillors was now under review because there had been many successful appeals and it was seen as too harsh.

Respondents identified the following issues associated with exclusion policies:

- It was felt almost universally that there was a need for greater information sharing between landlords operating in a particular locality, but at the same time there was a need to be vigilant about confidentiality considerations and data protection. One organisation gave an example of how there had been problems with defence lawyers arguing that information they were using against their client should not have been made available by the police under the Data Protection Act. There were similarities with the police in the differences between verbal informal sharing of information between housing officers, compared with formal, on the record, information in writing. Most seemed to suggest that if asked they would give information to organisations, even to the private sector. One officer spoke about doing this only when there had been a conviction or court case.

- In low demand areas or where there is a choice of social housing providers, excluding households can further weaken or diminish demand

and result in increasing levels of vacant property. It also has led to some frustration caused when registered social landlords may house someone without enquiring too much about them rather than leave another property empty.

> "There is a need for everybody to be working along the same lines. It is frustrating sometimes when people get rehoused, sometimes by another RSL, and that RSL has not bothered to check out with us the conduct of their tenancy when they've taken them on board. I don't know if that's to fill a low demand property or whatever, but it's frustrating and it can cause a serious problem if it happens to be very close to where they were living before."

On the other hand, there was also a feeling that this could work the other way, with at least one officer of a registered social landlord feeling that they were used deliberately as a dumping ground by local authorities for those that they had evicted, without passing on this information, especially where the household had vulnerable children.

- It was suggested that common housing registers and joint exclusion lists would be a good deterrent because people are less likely to be able to just, *"go round the corner and get another property"*, particularly in areas of low demand, where possession action maybe has less of an impact as it might in other areas. However, only in one case study area was there a joint exclusion list and a common housing register. One front line officer working in the North expressed the views of many:

> "Each local authority has got their own waiting list and their own register and it looks as though each local authority is having its own exclusion policy and each local authority is jealously guarding the details of those people who get excluded from their lists...Officially...Unofficially the housing officers do tend to talk to each other. But what I would want to see is the housing authorities all working together to send a message out and say to people, 'you know, if you cause problems in one local authority area then you can't expect to move to another local authority area and get rehoused'."

- Although local authorities who do have exclusion lists may not necessarily nominate anyone that they have previously excluded, it was felt that they don't always share information with registered social landlords, although this was improving.

> "I think what I have seen is there is more of an openness about sharing information. I think in the past it might have been the case you sign somebody up and 'oh, we're thinking of offering your tenant this property, what sort of

tenant have they been?' And you might not always get the truth because it's like, 'thank goodness, you know they're going, we don't want them either'. And I think I can certainly sense a change there. I'd say we've done this in the past, but we are much more honest now, we will be quite frank with people."

One of the suggestions for improvement here was the need for a nationwide register of households evicted or excluded for anti-social behaviour, along with the need for a tightening up of requirements for applicants to disclose full information of any incidence of anti-social behaviour. Another suggestion was for closer working between the smaller registered social landlords and the allocation teams of local authorities in order to provide appropriate support and make more appropriate allocations.

❑ Summary

Many officers recognised that eviction may simply displace the problem, and sometimes did not even achieve that as families moved back into the same area. One response to this is the use of exclusion lists. It is apparent that there is a growing trend for social landlords to exclude households on the grounds of anti-social behaviour. Around a half of all social landlords were found to have formal exclusion policies with nearly twice as many metropolitan authorities excluding households as compared to non-metropolitan authorities.

The criteria for exclusion varied widely between organisations. A number of problems were noted with such policies. For example, in unpopular areas, excluding households could contribute to a further weakening of demand and could result in increasing levels of empty property. Landlords were also aware that exclusion policies could have the effect of displacing the problem to the private sector.

CHAPTER 14

CONCLUSIONS

The original brief for this study focussed on an evaluation of the reported incidence of anti-social behaviour amongst tenants of social landlords operating in England, and the use of legal remedies to deal with such problems. The study was also designed to examine the strengths and weaknesses of current legal remedies, taking into account the views and experiences of housing professionals, lawyers and tenants – complainants and defendants – who had been centrally involved in anti-social behaviour cases. The lack of a nationally recognised system of classifying, recording and monitoring complaints means that it is simply not possible to verify the scale of the problem or to assess whether it is one which is increasing or not. Nevertheless, the research provides a useful benchmark in identifying the way in which landlords are seeking to develop effective ways of dealing with this complex and dynamic issue.

The report has been written at the same time as Policy Action Team 8 (PAT) of the Social Exclusion Unit (SEU) has been examining anti-social behaviour. We were pleased to be able to feed some of the findings from our work into their study, and many of their recommendations echo our own. Given the limited remit and timing of our study (see p. 10 of the Introduction, above), we have not examined the use of anti-social behaviour orders. They are dealt with at greater length by the SEU report (SEU, 2000), although comments made in the course of our study did indicate that for many practitioners on the ground, particularly in registered social landlords, they did not understand how anti-social behaviour orders worked, nor how they could access those who could make them work.

Landlords now have extensive legal powers to tackle neighbour nuisance. While some improvements may be needed in the court management of cases, the research found little evidence to support the view that further legal reform is required. Notices of Seeking Possession can be effective in stopping offending behaviour and where possession action is taken, the courts are most likely to grant landlords outright orders. Equally, the courts are sympathetic to granting injunctions as a method of dealing with anti-social behaviour. The evidence suggests that legal remedies have an important role to play in a neighbour nuisance strategy but that they are not appropriate in the majority of cases.

The development of wider strategies to deal with anti-social behaviour requires a greater understanding of the dynamic nature of the problem. Simple solutions are rarely sufficient. Anti-social behaviour can take many forms. Some incidents can be relatively minor, others very serious, causing extreme distress and misery to many people. The underlying causes are frequently complex and behaviours are likely to change over time.

While landlords are clearly willing to resort to possession action, many were aware that such action was only partially effective. It might sort out the problem locally, but there was a strong chord resonating throughout the interviews of eviction effectively being a 'failure'. What many people really needed was a range of support services coupled with improved housing management.

> "Everybody gets scared off. They don't want to work together and if, if somebody offers me a person that's got a problem then I think twice about that. I ask them what sort of support this person's got and things like that. And you get all sorts of promises. But at the end of the day, very rarely do they get that support. They're sort of semi-dumped. And I think that's a crying shame. I've had these people who are care in the community. They need more help, they need more help. It doesn't work."

As the number of complaints made has increased, landlords have responded by developing detailed operational procedures. But the research illustrates the difficulties landlords continue to experience in managing neighbour nuisance and anti-social behaviour cases. While some organisations have established specialist units/officers to develop and implement anti-social behaviour policies, many landlords felt there was a need for greater clarification of the range of action that could be taken to deal effectively with the different categories of disputes and nuisance. It was also recognised that there is a need for longer-term, multi agency strategies to address the behavioural problems often associated with anti-social behaviour. As one officer explained:

> "I think the Crime and Disorder Act is brilliant. If you couple that with the Protection from Harassment Act, it gives you all that you need to deal with nuisance. But it still comes down to the commitment of individuals and it shouldn't be. I don't know how you do it, if you have like secondments, having police working in the housing department and housing officers working in the police. So you can share that information. That's a much more close working."

In the absence of systems to promote joined up thinking and joined up action, methods of dealing with individual households may not be effective in the long-term and may indeed contribute to the development of more intransigent problems within the community as a whole.

Further evidence of the need for improved management of cases is provided by the analysis of complainants' and defendants' experiences. Although some landlords were developing the appropriate specialist skills, all too often tenants were disappointed by their landlords' response and thought more effective action could have been taken at an earlier stage.

Many complainants endure prolonged periods of anxiety and stress whilst seeking a resolution of problems. Acting as witnesses in injunction or possession proceedings requires great courage and it is often difficult for landlords to persuade neighbours to agree to give formal evidence. Complainants need to be confident that the landlord is taking the issue seriously and trying to stop the disturbing behaviour. Where complainants are provided with ongoing support and protection from witness intimidation they are more likely to be prepared to attend court hearings.

Defendants' criticisms of the way in which their case had been managed also underlines the importance of specialist training of housing officers to enable them to act in a professional manner when confronted with conflicting accounts of events. The study highlights the need for landlords to ensure that housing officers have the skills, knowledge and resources to be able to undertake thorough investigations and decide what action to take. Without such specialist skills there is a danger that inappropriate action many be taken causing distress and frustration to all involved.

Policy and practice needs to be directed towards the following areas:

■ Measurement and monitoring of the problem

- There is an urgent need for landlords to develop clear procedures for recording complaints and monitoring action taken to resolve problems. Without such systems it is impossible to establish the scale of the problem, assess whether it is increasing or decreasing, map alternative strategies and evaluate forms of intervention.

- Monitoring schemes need to be sufficiently sophisticated to identify the resource implications of different forms of action.

- Common systems of recording, categorising and monitoring complaints should be adopted by all landlords in order for both local and national audits of anti-social behaviour to be undertaken.

- Where households are evicted or excluded from social housing, landlords should record the number of people excluded and monitor the impact of such policies.

■ Development of multi-agency responses

- Dealing with anti-social behaviour frequently requires a multi-agency response. Such work is time consuming and can be difficult, if not impossible, for front line housing officers to achieve without the support of senior management in all the agencies concerned. Inter-agency co-operation needs to be developed at both strategic and operational levels.

- The development of the Crime and Disorder Partnerships provides a framework within which locally determined strategies can be developed. All key agencies should be encouraged to actively participate in the development of strategic responses to the issue.

- With the increasing diversity of landlords providing rented housing there is a danger that action taken by social landlords can simply displace the problem to the private sector. Strategies need to be developed which include private sector landlords within them.

- Given the high levels of vulnerability noted amongst perpetrators of anti-social behaviour, there is a need to develop closer working relationship between landlords, social service departments and other agencies providing support services.

- Improved information sharing protocols and the promotion of 'good practice' amongst agencies dealing with anti-social behaviour needs to be developed. The development of such protocols should involve front line officers as well as senior managers.

■ Operational management

- Front line housing officers are usually the first point of contact in neighbour disputes. They must be able to respond promptly by undertaking thorough investigation before deciding on appropriate action.

- While most organisations have anti-social behaviour procedures and provide officers with some training on the use of legal remedies many officers lack confidence about handling such cases. Ongoing, specialist training is required to ensure that housing officers collect and evaluate evidence, are equipped to take witness statements, and provide witnesses with support.

- Dealing with anti-social behaviour is time consuming and requires a high level of knowledge and skill. Specialist teams/officers, can provide both practical support and ongoing training and skills development for front line officers and the provision of such services should be encouraged.

- Witness support measures need to be developed by many landlords. In addition to maintaining close contact with potential witnesses by regular visits, practical measures such as accompanied visits to court prior to the formal hearing, the provision of mobile phones, alarms and if necessary the provision of temporary accommodation should be considered.

- Many landlords are developing innovative strategies to deal with particular problems of neighbour nuisance but there is frequently little research undertaken into the impact of different initiatives. Further research to evaluate such strategies is essential in order to establish the wider applicability of innovations and 'good practice'.

■ Use of existing legal remedies

- Prior to taking the decision to issue a Notice of Seeking Possession, individual cases should be fully investigated with personal visits to take statements from both the complainants and the alleged perpetrators.

- All Notices of Seeking Possession served on the grounds of anti-social behaviour should, where possible, be personally served on tenants rather than sent through the post or hand delivered.

- In appropriate cases, landlords should be encouraged to consider use of suspended possession orders, rather than automatically seeking outright orders.

- If landlords are to be encouraged to make greater use of injunctions as a method of dealing with anti-social behaviour, there is a need for improved information dissemination about the benefits of such an approach.

- Increased provision of ongoing training for lawyers and housing officers in the application and operation of injunctions should be a priority for staff development.

■ Court administration of cases

- Despite the recent changes to court administration introduced following the Woolf report (1996), there is evidence that courts do not always take into account the particular problems associated with anti-social behaviour cases. Landlords should take an active part in court users' groups in order to improve courts' understanding and management of cases.

- There are frequently long delays in obtaining court hearings. In possession actions it was not uncommon for cases to take nine months from issuing a summons to final trial. Such delays could prejudice cases with potential witnesses dropping out the longer the delay in obtaining a final hearing. Courts should give greater priority to the early listing of anti-social behaviour cases.

- The level of knowledge and the skill of the judiciary in dealing with serious anti-social behaviour cases varies from court to court. Guidance notes and training should be made available to judges and they should be encouraged to adopt Lord Woolf's recommended approach to visit local estates and talk to residents.

■ Witness protection measures

- A victim-centred approach to witnesses in anti-social behaviour cases needs to be developed by courts, with for example, the provision of separate waiting areas for witnesses and defendants.

- In order to reduce the intimidating experience of giving formal evidence consideration should be given to holding hearings in judges' private chambers rather than in open court.

■ Legal Aid

- The availability of Legal Aid for defendants in anti-social behaviour cases varies from one area to another. Guidance notes should be provided to regional Legal Aid Boards to ensure a consistency of approach and to minimise delays in dealing with such applications.

REFERENCES

Atkinson R, Mullen T and Scott S (2000) *The Use of Civil Legal Remedies for Neighbour Nuisance in Scotland*. Edinburgh: Scottish Executive Central Research Unit.

Chartered Institute of Housing (1998) *Good Practice Briefing, Neighbour Nuisance: New Initiatives*. Coventry: Chartered Institute of Housing.

Cole I, Kane S and Robinson D (1999) *Changing Demand, Changing Neighbourhoods: The Response of Social Landlords*. Sheffield Hallam University: CRESR.

Department of Environment (1993) *Managing Social Housing*. London: HMSO.

Department of the Environment (1994) R*ent Arrears in Local Authorities and Housing Associations in England*. London: HMSO.

Department of the Environment (1995) *Anti-social Behaviour on Housing Estates: Consultation Paper on Probationary Tenancies*. London: DoE.

Department of Environment/Department of Health (1997) *Code of Guidance on the Housing Act 1996, Parts VI and VII*. London: DoE.

Department of Environment Transport and the Regions (1999) *Report by the Unpopular Housing Action Team*. London: DETR.

Dhooge T and Barelli J (1996) *Racial Attacks and Harassment: the response of Social Landlords*. London Research Centre/Department of Environment. London: HMSO.

Dignan J, Sorsby A and Hibbert J (1996) *Neighbour Disputes: Comparing the Cost-effectiveness of Mediation and Alternative Approaches*. Sheffield: Sheffield Centre for Criminological and Legal Research, University of Sheffield.

Housing Corporation (1998) *Performance Standards: Performance Standards and Regulatory Guidance for Registered Social Landlords*. London: Housing Corporation.

Housing Corporation (1999) *Performance Standards, Addendum 4 to the Social Housing Standards for General and Supported Housing: Anti-Social Behaviour*. London: Housing Corporation.

Hunter C, Mullen T with Scott S (1998) *Legal Remedies for Neighbour Nuisance: Comparing Scottish and English Approaches*. York: York Publishing Services.

Hunter C (2000) 'Dealing with anti-social behaviour: tenancy terms and conditions'. *Journal of Housing Law*, pp 3-7.

Labour Party (1995) *A Quiet Life: Tough Action on Criminal Neighbours*. London: Labour Party.

Legal Aid Board Franchise Development Group (2000) 'Board organises CLS seminars'. *Legal Action*, January, p 5.

Manning J (1998) 'Reasonableness: A New Approach', *Journal of Housing Law*, pp 59-62.

Nixon J, Hunter C and Shayer S (1999) *The Use of Legal Remedies by social Landlords to deal with Neighbour Nuisance*. Sheffield Hallam University: CRESR.

Papps P (1998) 'Anti-social Behaviour Strategies – Individualistic or Holistic?' *Housing Studies*, Vol 13: 5 pp. 639-656.

Ruggieri S and Levison D (1998) *Starter Tenancies and Introductory Tenancies: An Evaluation*. London: Housing Corporation.

Smith N and George C (1997) 'Introductory tenancies: a nuisance too far?' *Journal of Social Welfare and Family Law*, Vol 19: 3, pp. 307-20.

Social Exclusion Unit (2000) *Report of Policy Action Team 8: Anti-social behaviour*. London: Social Exclusion Unit.

Woolf (1996) *Access to Justice Final Report*. London: HMSO.

APPENDIX 1

THE STUDY METHODOLOGY

■ Questionnaire data

From a database of all English local authorities we selected those who were known to have housing departments. This excluded all county councils and those where a complete stock transfer had taken place. For the registered social landlords (RSLs) a database of all those with general needs stock (as defined by the Housing Corporation) over 500 units was obtained.

We divided the RSLs into three types: large scale voluntary transfers (LSVTs), RSLs (not including LSVTs) over 10,000 units, and RSLs (not including LSVTs) under 10,000 units. This division was adopted because we thought it would be useful to see if there were any differences in problem or approach according to stock size. We made a separate category of the LSVTs, because the stock and management were more likely to be shaped by their local authority origins. Local authorities were broken down into four types: London boroughs, metropolitan, non-metropolitan and unitary authorities. Again, we felt these had particular characteristics worth separating. London was felt to be a unique entity which created potentially different dynamics. Metropolitan authorities covered other large scale urban areas, were most likely to have the largest numbers of stock, and to be the site of some of the worst estate housing and associated social problems. We also divided all organisations into regions, as defined by the Department of the Environment, Transport and Regions (DETR), and five different stock size categories (see Appendix 2).

Grouped alphabetically in types and regions, we then created our final structured sample by selecting two out of every three organisations. We were looking for a maximum initial sample of around 400, which, with a response rate of at least 60 per cent, would give us a large enough final sample. Questionnaires were sent to 200 local authorities (including five Housing Action Trusts (HATS)) and 188 registered social landlords.

269 organisations responded out of a total of 388, making a combined response rate of 69 per cent. There was a 71 per cent response rate from local authorities, with 141 answering out of 200. 128 RSLs responded out of 188 contacted, making a 68 per cent response rate. Three HATs responded out of the five contacted. In order to ensure our final set of responses were representative of the different categories mentioned above, a balanced telephone follow-up was done of those who had not responded to improve the response rate. The high response rate combined with the representative nature of the survey sample increases the reliability and validity of the survey findings.

The full break down of the response rate according to these categories can be found in Appendix 3. There were no significant variations of response amongst the range and type of landlord nor amongst the regions. Across all landlords it was those in the London region (63 per cent) and in the South East (64 per cent) who were the lowest responders, compared with those in Yorkshire and Humberside, the best by far at 83 per cent. There were no noticeable exceptions amongst local authorities specifically, apart from only a 60 per cent response rate from metropolitan authorities in the North West.

There was more variation amongst the RSLs. The lowest response rate according to type of RSLs was from the main group, (RSLs (not including LSVTs) with under 10,000 dwellings), at only 63 per cent, with LSVTs being the highest respondents of all landlords, at 81 per cent. Those who responded least on a regional basis varied according to type of organisation, e.g. only 52 per cent of the main group of RSLs responded in the North West, and only 53 per cent in the West Midlands. With one exception, there were also no noticeable differences according to stock size. Amongst those RSLs with stock between 4,500 and 9,999 there was only a 48 per cent response rate.

It should also be borne in mind that there was a variable rate of responses to individual questions. The questionnaire required respondents to provide detailed information on a range of legal remedies. Most landlords could answer some but not all of the questions. As a result, the number of respondents for each question is not consistent, but varies from one question to another.

■ Sub-samples

In order to facilitate analysis of the survey data two sub-samples were created, which enabled the detailed responses on the use and effectiveness of different legal remedies to be examined more closely.

Sub-sample 1

First, we drew on the data provided by a sub-sample of landlords made up of organisations whose record keeping and monitoring systems were sufficiently sophisticated to enable them to provide comprehensive data over the period 1996/97 and 1997/98. Sub-sample 1 comprised 16 per cent of the sample of RSLs and 22 per cent of LAs for the period 1996/97, but by the following year increased to 41 per cent of LAs and 26 per cent RSLs. Data from sub-sample 1 was analysed in terms of the number of cases in which NSPs, possession proceedings and/or injunctions had been issued, and the legal outcomes of such actions. An assessment was then made of the effectiveness of these remedies in preventing the need for further legal action, although it is acknowledged that only a minority of the total sample were able to provide this level of detail for individual cases.

The characteristics of sub-sample 1 were cross referenced with the characteristics of the main sample, in order to check the validity of the sampling method. The sub-sample was found to be representative of the main sample of landlords in most respects, for example, in terms of the size, geographical location and type of RSL. The only major difference identified was that sub-sample 1 included a higher proportion of metropolitan authorities and the London boroughs than the main sample.

Data from sub-sample 1 has been used to analyse the possession process and the detailed outcomes of cases. These findings suggest that landlords' use of different legal remedies is changing. However, the data from this sub-sample is not sensitive to possible differences in the way landlords use legal remedies according to size or type of the organisation.

Sub-sample 2

A more reliable method of comparing results across organisations with different stock sizes, was obtained by analysing the survey findings in terms of the incidence and use of different legal remedies per 1,000 tenancies. Sub-sample 2 was made up of those landlords who were able to provide information on the number of tenancies managed, the number of complaints recorded, the overall number of NSPs issued and the number of cases in which possession action was commenced. The recorded complaint level, the number of NSPs issued, and the level of possession actions per 1,000 tenancies was then computed in order to obtain a data set that was robust enough to be subject to comparative analysis. We have some caveats about these figures, however. Sub-sample 2 comprised a larger sample of landlords than in sub-sample 1, but it was rare for respondents to achieve a 100 per cent completion rate for all the survey questions. In most instances, organisations could provide some but not all of the required data, therefore the number of organisations included in sub-sample 2 who responded to each question varies.

Throughout the report the term 'average' refers to the median average rather than the mean average which can be affected by extreme values in the distribution of responses.

■ Case studies

Five areas were chosen for the case studies. The areas were chosen in order to provide a range of geographical locations including a contrast between those with a high demand for social housing and those facing low demand. In addition, account was taken of the existence of pioneering methods of dealing with the problem and the sample was constructed to include a range of different social landlord types including a large metropolitan authority, different sized RSLs and an area where all the council stock had been transferred under the LSVT provisions.

In each case study area, two landlords, a local authority and a RSL, were identified and agreed to take part in the study. Information was gathered by way of interviews and by asking each landlord to provide the case files (both housing and legal) for up to five nuisance cases which had proceeded to a variety of stages, within the last three years. Interview schedules were prepared and a proforma for gathering information from the case files. These were piloted in Sheffield and subsequently refined. Following the pilot, it was decided not to seek information on the individual cases from the court files since these did not appear to offer any substantial further information.

In each area, we sought interviews with a senior and front line housing officer for each landlord, their legal representative, a tenant complainant, a defence lawyer and a local judge. It has not proved possible to undertake a complete set of interviews in some areas since in some it was not possible to identify a defence lawyer with sufficient experience, and in one the landlord had just changed their own lawyer. Further, obtaining permission to interview judges from the Lord Chancellor's department has proved difficult and time consuming, and it has not proved possible to identify a judge in all areas. In fact, only two interviews have been completed. We also sought interviews with tenant defendants but these have proved difficult to arrange (see further below).

The landlords involved, geographic areas and interviews completed are shown in the following table:

Case study area	Type of landlord	Who has been interviewed
Large metropolitan conurbation in the North West	Manchester City Council	Senior officer, front line officer, lawyer, tenant complainant
	Guinness Housing Trust	Senior officer, front line officer, private sector lawyer, tenant complainant, judge, defence lawyer
Mixed urban/rural area in the West Midlands	Stoke on Trent City Council	Senior officer (x2), front line officer, lawyer and legal executive, tenant complainant
	Staffordshire HA	Senior officer, front line officer, private sector lawyer, tenant complainant, defence lawyer, judge
Medium sized borough council and RSL operating in a mixed urban/rural area in the North East	Hartlepool Borough Council	Senior officer, front line officer, lawyer, tenant complainant
	Three Rivers HA	Senior officer, front line officer, tenant complainant
LSVT and RSL operating in the South West	Magna HA (LSVT)	Senior officer, front line officer, lawyer, tenant complainant, tenant defendant
	Raglan HA	Senior officer, front line officer, private sector lawyer, defence para-legal
Inner London borough with TEST	Lewisham LBC	Senior officer, front line officer, lawyer
	Hexagon HA	TEST (x2), front line officer, private sector lawyer, tenant complainant

The eight complainants interviewed were drawn from a range of household types. Brief details of their household composition and the length of their tenancy are:

- Two middle aged women living in nearby properties. Both women had families and had lived in the same area for many years.

- A couple in their late 20s occupying a flat on a small housing association estate.

- An elderly single woman who suffered from health problems. She had rented the property for many years prior to purchasing the flat under the Right to Buy regulations.

- A couple with two teenage children who had lived in the same property for over 16 years.

- A young single man who was a tenant member of the landlord's governing body. He had lived in the flat for three years.

- A couple in their late 50s who had moved into a new-build property when it was first let a number of years earlier.

- A couple with two young children who had bought the property seven years prior to the nuisance behaviour commencing.

- A couple with one young child who had been long-term tenants of the landlord.

Because of the difficulties identifying potential perpetrators who were willing to be interviewed in the case study areas, we also pursued other access to such interviewees. Through a para-legal who had worked for the Legal Services Trust we were offered the opportunity to interview five tenants, all living in the North West, but not within a case study area, who had had legal action taken against them. To increase the number of interviews with legal representatives, we also interviewed the para-legal who had worked on the cases, and also a lawyer with extensive experience of working for social landlords throughout England on anti-social behaviour cases.

Details of the defendants interviewed are as follows:

- A single teenage woman.

- A single mother in her late 20s, with two young children.

- An elderly couple in their mid 60s. The man had recently suffered a stroke and suffered from other ailments. The woman had suffered from depression since their grandchildren were killed in a fire a couple of years previously followed by the death of their son (the father of the children), and had received psychiatric care, and was generally of poor health. They had lived in the same street for over 30 years, without previous incident.

- The daughter of the above couple who was in her mid 20s, with a five year old daughter. The woman was a heroin addict and had lived in the same street all her life.

- A couple in their early 50s, both suffering from medical depression and other health problems, with an 18 year old daughter with learning difficulties and 21 year old son. The man was unable to work for health reasons. They have been council tenants for over 24 years with no prior complaints about anti-social behaviour.

- A couple in their 40s, with the woman suffering from multiple sclerosis, angina, hearing loss and other health and psychiatric problems. Both had been tenants of the same housing association for around 10 years with no previous reports of anti-social behaviour.

■ Case files

The defendant survey sample consisted of 62 nuisance cases selected by the ten case study landlords and the pilot case study landlord, plus the five cases provided through the para-legal, giving a total sample of 67 defendants. Thus, the sample was drawn from a variety of social landlords operating in a range of geographical locations, including areas with a high demand for social housing and those facing low demand. The tenure of households in the sample was equally spilt between LAs and RSLs with 50 per cent (33) of households renting from RSLs and 50 per cent (34) LAs. In selecting the individual cases to be included in the case file survey, landlords were asked to include cases which had proceeded to a variety of pre-court and court stages, and where action had been taken within the last three years. In the majority of cases, data was collected from tenancy files and subsequently cross referenced with the legal files. The quality of this information varied considerably; in some cases comprehensive information was detailed in the files, whilst in others the information recorded appeared to be incomplete or may have been subject to some filtering by the landlord.

APPENDIX 2

STOCK SIZE CATEGORIES AND REGIONS USED IN THE SURVEY

(as defined by the Department of the Environment, Transport and the Regions)

Stock size breakdown and code used for RSLs

500 – 1,499	=	1
1,500 – 2,499	=	2
2,500 – 4,499	=	3
4,500 – 9,999	=	4
over 10,000	=	5

Stock size breakdown and code used for LAs

500 – 3,999	=	1
4,000 – 7,999	=	2
8,000 – 14,999	=	3
15,000 – 29,999	=	4
over 30,000	=	5

North West (NW):
Cheshire, Cumbria, Greater Manchester and Lancashire

Yorkshire and Humberside (YH):
North Yorkshire, South Yorkshire, West Yorkshire and Humberside

North East (NE):
Cleveland, Durham, Northumberland, Teesside and Tyne and Wear

East Midlands (EM):
Derbyshire, Leicestershire, Lincolnshire, Northamptonshire, Nottinghamshire and Rutland

West Midlands (WM):

Metropolitan districts of Birmingham, Coventry, Dudley, Sandwell, Solihull, Walsall and Wolverhampton; and the counties of Worcestershire, Shropshire, Staffordshire and Warwickshire; and the unitary authority of Herefordshire

South East (SE):

Berkshire, Buckinghamshire, Hampshire, Isle of Wight, Kent, Oxfordshire, Surrey, East Sussex and West Sussex

East (E):

Bedfordshire, Cambridgeshire, Essex, Hertfordshire, Norfolk and Suffolk

South West (SW):

Unitary authorities of Bath and North East Somerset, Bristol, North Somerset and South Gloucestershire; and the counties of Cornwall and Isles of Scilly, Devon, Dorset, Gloucestershire, Somerset and Wiltshire

London (L):

Greater London

Appendix 3

Response Rate According to Regions and Organisation Type

Response rate according to region and organisation type

Responses			Number in total sample			Response rate
Type	Region	Total	Type	Region	Total	
Large RSLs	E	0	Large RSLs	E	1	0.00%
	L	2		L	3	66.67%
	NW	2		NW	2	100.00%
	SE	2		SE	3	66.67%
	WM	1		WM	1	100.00%
Large RSLs TOTAL		**7**	**Large RSLs TOTAL**		**10**	**70.00%**
LSVTs	E	4	LSVTs	E	5	80.00%
	L	2		L	3	66.67%
	NW	3		NW	3	100.00%
	SE	14		SE	20	70.00%
	SW	6		SW	7	85.71%
	WM	7		WM	7	100.00%
	YH	2		YH	2	100.00%
LSVTs TOTAL		**38**	**LSVTs TOTAL**		**47**	**80.85%**
Rest of RSLs	E	9	Rest of RSLs	E	12	75.00%
	EM	3		EM	6	50.00%
	L	22		L	37	59.46%
	NE	5		NE	5	100.00%
	NW	11		NW	21	52.38%
	SE	9		SE	16	56.25%
	SW	7		SW	8	87.50%
	WM	8		WM	15	53.33%
	YH	9		YH	11	81.82%
Rest of RSLs TOTAL		**83**	**Rest of RSLs TOTAL**		**131**	**63.36%**

Responses			Number in total sample			Response rate
Type	Region	Total	Type	Region	Total	
London boroughs	L	13	London boroughs	L	19	68.42%
	SE	1		SE	2	50.00%
London boroughs TOTAL		**14**	**London boroughs TOTAL**		**21**	**66.67%**
Metropolitan	NE	2	Metropolitan	NE	3	66.67%
	NW	6		NW	10	60.00%
	WM	3		WM	4	75.00%
	YH	5		YH	6	83.33%
Metropolitan TOTAL		**16**	**Metropolitan TOTAL**		**23**	**69.57%**
Non-metropolitan	E	15	Non-metropolitan	E	24	62.50%
	EM	16		EM	23	69.57%
	NE	7		NE	10	70.00%
	NW	11		NW	13	84.62%
	SE	16		SE	23	69.57%
	SW	11		SW	16	68.75%
	WM	9		WM	12	75.00%
	YH	2		YH	3	66.67%
Non-metropolitan TOTAL		**87**	**Non-metropolitan TOTAL**		**124**	**70.16%**
Unitaries	E	2	Unitaries	E	3	66.67%
	EM	4		EM	4	100.00%
	NE	3		NE	3	100.00%
	NW	2		NW	3	66.67%
	SE	3		SE	6	50.00%
	SW	3		SW	4	75.00%
	WM	2		WM	2	100.00%
	YH	2		YH	2	100.00%
Unitaries TOTAL		**21**	**Unitaries TOTAL**		**27**	**77.78%**
Housing Action Trust (HAT)	n/a	3	Housing Action Trust (HAT)	n/a	5	60.00%
HAT TOTAL		**3**	**HAT TOTAL**		**5**	**60.00%**
GRAND TOTAL		**269**	**GRAND TOTAL**		**388**	**69.33%**

OTHER BOOKS PUBLISHED BY THE CHARTERED INSTITUTE OF HOUSING FOR THE JOSEPH ROWNTREE FOUNDATION

Housing Sex Offenders – An examination of current practice

Dave Cowan, Rose Gilroy, Mark Bevan and Christina Pantazis

The question of how society deals with the rehousing of sex offenders has raised considerable anxiety. This report looks at how sex offenders have been rehoused in three different areas and how community safety objectives have been met, covering issues such as:
- role of housing professionals in multi-agency partnerships
- involving housing providers in risk assessment
- housing's role in managing sex offenders in the community.

Semi-structured and confidential interviews allowed the researchers to get to the heart of the dilemmas and difficult choices faced by professionals.

Price: £13.95   ISBN: 1 900396 04 1   Published: October 1999

Low Demand – Separating fact from fiction

Alan Holmans and Merron Simpson

What is the truth behind the debate about abandonment of housing in the north and unparalleled demand in the south? National projections only give half the picture. This study looks at what is happening in each region, and also includes case studies of five local areas. By examining population trends and indicators of demand at all levels, it separates fact from fiction.

Price: £13.95   ISBN: 1 900396 63 7   Published: June 1999

Accounting for the Uncountable – Tenant participation in housing modernisation

Ian Cole, Paul Hickman and Barbara Reid

Tenant involvement and choice in housing modernisation are now firmly established. How do social landlords make decisions about involving tenants? Based on four case studies, the authors analyse the process and look at costs and benefits. An invaluable aid for those developing tenant compacts for modernisation projects.

Is accompanied by a CD ROM which provides a practical guide through the issues involved in building tenant participation into housing modernisation.

Report price: £13.95   ISBN: 1 900396 33 5   Published: June 1999

CD ROM price: £25.00   ISBN: 1 900396 29 7   Published: January 2000

Local Housing Companies – Progress and problems

Brendan Nevin

Six councils set out to create the first local housing companies by transferring estates in their areas. What was the outcome? This study, by an author involved in one of the planned transfers, looks at experience in developing the pioneering housing companies, what led to either success or failure, and what can be learnt for future transfers in urban areas.

Price: £12.95   ISBN: 1 900396 73 4   Published: June 1999

Digital Futures – Making homes smarter

David Gann, James Barlow and Tim Venables

Are we on the threshold of a completely new approach to the way the environment in our homes is controlled? The study argues that our use of technology in the home is about to take a leap forward – and it shows exactly where we might be heading. Based on experience with two pilot projects, it describes a digital future in which we will have Smart Homes that can be programmed to give us the environment we want using domestic devices in much more intelligent ways.

The video provides an accessible introduction to the idea of Smart Homes. It includes interviews with some of the participants in the project and a look at how the project has been piloted. Viewers can see what a Smart Home might actually look like!

The CD ROM provides accessible technical material for those wanting to have more detail about how Smart Homes might be created.

Book price: £12.95   ISBN: 1 900396 73 4   Published: October 1999

Video price: £9.95 inc VAT   ISBN: 1 900396 19 X

CD ROM price: £13.95 inc VAT   ISBN: 1 900396 24 6

Special Offer for all three (book, video, CD ROM): £25 inc VAT (also includes p&p)

Also available in the CIH/JRF series:

Housing Associations and Rent Arrears – Attitudes, beliefs and behaviour
Price: £13.95   ISBN: 1 900396 92 0

Working with Young People on Estates: the role of housing professionals in multi-agency work
Price: £10.95   ISBN: 1 900396 87 4

Pick and Mix: Developing flexible housing choices in community care
Price: £13.95   ISBN: 1 900396 62 9

Energy Advice to Tenants – Does it work?
Price: £13.95   ISBN: 1 900396 56 4

Child's Play: Facilitating Play on Housing Estates
Price: £9.95   ISBN: 900396 26 2

Creating Communities or Welfare Housing? – A study of new housing association developments in Yorkshire/Humberside
Price: £13.95   ISBN: 900396 75 0

And published jointly by CIH and CML for the Joseph Rowntree Foundation:
Housing Finance Review 1999/2000
Price £25.00   ISBN 1 900396 88 2

Further information on all the above from:
Publications,
Chartered Institute of Housing,
Octavia House, Westwood Way,
Coventry, CV4 8JP.
Tel: 024 7685 1764. Fax: 024 7642 2022.
E-mail: pubs@cih.org